CW00480897

Diabetic Air Fryer

Cookbook for Beginners UK

1600 Days of Tasty and Nourishing Air-Fried Recipes for Beginners and Pros, 28-Day Meal Plan to Manage Blood Sugar Levels and Promote Overall Wellness

Evie Vincent

All Rights Reserved.

The content contained within this book may not be reproduced, duplicated, or transmitted without direct written permission from the author or the publisher. Under no circumstances will any blame or legal responsibility be held against the publisher, or author, for any damages, reparation, or monetary loss due to the information contained within this book, either directly or indirectly.

Legal Notice: This book is copyright protected. It is only for personal use. You cannot amend, distribute, sell, use, quote or paraphrase any part, or the content within this book, without the consent of the author or publisher.

Disclaimer Notice:

Please note the information contained within this document is for educational and entertainment purposes only. All effort has been executed to present accurate, up to date, reliable, complete information. No warranties of any kind are declared or implied. Readers acknowledge that the author is not engaged in the rendering of legal, financial, medical, or professional advice. The content within this book has been derived from various sources. Please consult a licensed professional before attempting any techniques outlined in this book. By reading this document, the reader agrees that under no circumstances is the author responsible for any losses, direct or indirect, that are incurred as a result of the use of the information contained within this document, including, but not limited to, errors, omissions, or inaccuracies.

CONTENTS

Other Favorite Recipes 63

Appendix : Recipes Index 75

Hi, I'm Evie Vincent, a home cook on a culinary quest, but due to my diabetes, I was often unable to eat the food I wanted to eat, and looking at the delicious food that came out of the air fryer, I had to look away, but I didn't want to give up, and after reviewing various sources, I gradually came up with an air fryer cookbook for diabetics, a groundbreaking cookbook designed for individuals managing diabetes and those seeking healthier food choices. A groundbreaking cooking guide designed for individuals managing diabetes and those seeking healthier food choices. 1600 air fryer recipes specially developed for diabetics, with 28-day meal plans to help you eat healthy and delicious.

Built on the principle of balancing flavor and nutrition, this cookbook embraces the incredible versatility of the air fryer, a kitchen tool that guarantees mouth-watering meals with a fraction of the fat and calories found in traditional cooking methods. The Diabetic Air Fryer Diet Cookbook is your gateway to a vast array of recipes that maintain stable blood sugar levels, promote weight management, and enhance overall well-being. If, like me, you experience diabetes and see delicious food but are afraid to eat it, then give this Diabetic Air Fryer diet Cookbook a try and embark on a journey of food freedom!

What is Diabetic?

Diabetes, a chronic metabolic disease that causes high blood sugar and the body's inability to properly regulate sugar distribution, symptoms of diabetes may include frequent urination, excessive thirst, unexplained weight loss, extreme hunger, etc. If not managed properly, diabetes can lead to serious complications such as heart disease, stroke, kidney disease, eye problems, dental disease, nerve damage and foot problems. It is therefore important for people diagnosed with diabetes to monitor their health and maintain a sensible diet.

Can diabetics eat air fryer food?

people with diabetes can eat air-fried food, and it can actually be a healthier alternative to traditional frying methods. Air fryers use hot air to cook food, which can give the food a similar texture to deep-fried food but without the extra oil and calories.

However, it's important to note what type of food is being air fried. For example, air-fried vegetables or lean proteins can be a healthy addition to a meal, while air-fried foods that are high in carbohydrates, like french fries or breaded items, should be consumed in moderation due to their potential impact on blood sugar levels.

In addition, many store-bought breadings and seasonings may contain added sugars or unhealthy fats, so it's best to use homemade seasoning mixes and avoid adding too much breading.

Remember, portion size is also key in managing blood sugar levels. Even healthier foods can lead to high blood sugar if eaten in large quantities. People with diabetes need to develop a meal plan that is appropriate to their individual nutritional needs and goals. This meal plan can certainly include fried foods, as long as they are prepared in a healthy way and eaten as part of a balanced diet.

What is the benefit of diabetic air fryer cookbook?

● A Diabetic Air Fryer Cookbook can offer numerous benefits, especially for those looking to manage their blood sugar levels while still enjoying a variety of tasty foods.

● Healthier Meals: Air fryers use hot air to cook food, which drastically reduces the need for oil. This results in meals that have less fat and fewer calories compared to traditionally fried foods, aiding in weight management and overall health.

● Nutrient Preservation: The rapid cooking time in air fryers often means that more nutrients are preserved in the food compared to other cooking methods, such as boiling or deep frying.

● Variety of Recipes: These cookbooks offer a wide range of recipes that cater to the dietary needs of people with diabetes. This can help add variety to your meals and prevent diet burnout.

● Portion Control: Recipes in these cookbooks are usually portioned out, helping you maintain control over serving sizes, which is crucial in managing blood glucose levels.

● Guideline: These cookbooks not only provide recipes, but they often also include educational information about managing diabetes, understanding how

different foods affect blood sugar levels, and tips for a balanced, nutritious diet.

● Encourages Home Cooking: By providing a range of tasty and easy-to-prepare recipes, the cookbook encourages more home cooking, where you have better control over the ingredients and portions, as opposed to eating out or ordering takeout.

How to maintain your air fryer?

Maintaining your air fryer not only ensures that it continues to function properly but also extends its lifespan. Here are some tips for maintaining your air fryer:

1.Clean After Every Use: It's important to clean your air fryer after each use to prevent buildup of food debris and oil. Allow the appliance to cool down before you start cleaning.

7. Regular Checks: Regularly check the air fryer for any damages such as a cracked or broken handle, issues with the cord, or non-functioning buttons. If you notice any faults, reach out to the manufacturer or a professional repair service.

8. Proper Storage: When not in use, store your air fryer in a clean, dry place. Make sure it is completely dry before storing to avoid bacteria and mold growth.

9. Follow the Manufacturer's Instructions: Always refer to the user manual or manufacturer's instructions for specific cleaning and maintenance advice for your particular model.

By properly maintaining your air fryer, you can ensure that it works efficiently and lasts for a long time. Enjoy the health and happiness of an air fryer!

2. Wash the Detachable Parts: Most air fryers come with detachable parts like the cooking basket, tray, and pan. These parts are usually dishwasher safe, but you can also hand wash them using warm soapy water. For stubborn food particles, soak the parts in warm soapy water for a while before scrubbing.

3. Clean the Inside: Wipe the inside of the air fryer with a damp cloth or sponge. Be careful not to scratch the interior surface. For stubborn grease, you can use a small amount of dish soap, but make sure to rinse and wipe it thoroughly.

4. Clean the Heating Element: The heating element should also be cleaned regularly to remove any food debris or grease that could potentially cause smoke or affect the appliance's performance. First, unplug the air fryer and ensure it is cool. Use a clean, dry brush to carefully remove any food particles or debris.

5. Wipe the Exterior: The outside of the air fryer can be wiped down with a damp cloth. If your air fryer is stainless steel, there are specific cleaning products available to give it a nice shine.

6. Don't Use Abrasive Tools: Avoid using metal utensils, abrasive cleaning pads, or harsh chemicals to clean your air fryer as these can damage the non-stick coating.

28-Day Meal Plan

Day	Breakfast	Lunch	Dinner
1	Pancakes 5	Herb Chicken Thighs 28	Sesame Seeds Coated Tuna 52
2	Cream Buns With Strawberries 5	Chicken Nuggets 29	Scallops With Creamy Tomato Sauce 52
3	Misto Quente 6	Cheesy Pork Chops In Air Fryer 29	Lime-garlic Shrimp Kebabs 53
4	Cauliflower Hash Browns 6	Tasty Harissa Chicken 30	Air-fried Fish Nuggets 53
5	Grilled Cheese 7	Pork Tenderloin With Mustard Glazed 30	Honey-glazed Salmon 54
6	Scotch Eggs 7	Air Fryer Hen Wings 31	Air Fried Cajun Salmon 54
7	Zucchini Bread 8	Air Fryer Bbq Cheddar-Stuffed Hen Breasts 31	Fish Finger Sandwich 54
8	Tofu Scramble 8	Crispy Chicken Thighs 32	Grilled Salmon With Lemon 55
9	Blueberry Buns 9	Chicken Wings 32	Salmon Cakes In Air Fryer 55
10	Blueberry Muffins 9	Lemon Pepper Chicken Breast 33	Salmon Patties 55
11	Bacon Bbq 10	Crumbed Poultry Tenderloins 33	Coconut Shrimp 56
12	Cocotte Eggs 10	Air Fryer Vegetables & Italian Sausage 34	Fish Sticks 56
13	Broccoli Mash 11	Fried Chicken Tamari And Mustard 34	Fish With Maille Dijon Originale Mustard 57
14	French Toast In Sticks 11	Chicken Tears 35	Basil-parmesan Crusted Salmon 57

Day	Breakfast	Lunch	Dinner
15	Breakfast Pizza 12	Southwest Chicken In Air Fryer 35	Salmon With Brown Sugar Glaze 58
16	Garlic Bread 12	Air Fryer Breaded Pork Chops 36	Lemon Garlic Shrimp In Air Fryer 58
17	Zucchini And Walnut Cake With Maple Flavor Icing 13	Chicken Wings With Garlic Parmesan 36	Mushrooms Stuffed With Tuna 59
18	Scallion Sandwich 13	Garlic-roasted Chicken With Creamer Potatoes 37	Breaded Hake 59
19	Tortilla 14	Crispy Ranch Air Fryer Nuggets 37	Crisped Flounder Fillet With Crumb Tops 59
20	Herb Frittata 14	No-breading Chicken Breast In Air Fryer 38	Salmon 60
21	Lean Lamb And Turkey Meatballs With Yogurt 15	Breaded Chicken Tenderloins 38	Crispy Fish Sandwiches 60
22	Chickpea, Tuna, And Kale Salad 15	Chicken Thighs 39	Air Fryer Fish & Chips 61
23	Vegan Breakfast Sandwich 16	Orange Chicken Wings 39	Baked Salmon 61
24	Easy Air Fryer Omelet 17	Chicken Bites In Air Fryer 39	Tilapia 62
25	Avocado Fries 17	Mini Apple Oat Muffins 40	Air Fryer Shrimp Scampi 62
26	Air Fryer Mini Pizza 19	Pork Rind 40	Air-fried Cinnamon Biscuit Bite 63
27	Keto French Fries 19	Short Ribs 41	Avocado White Bean Sandwich 63
28	Chicken Croquette 20	Diet Boiled Ribs 41	Creamy Halibut 66

BASIC KITCHEN CONVERSIONS & EQUIVALENTS

DRY MEASUREMENTS CONVERSION CHART

3 TEASPOONS = 1 TABLESPOON = 1/16 CUP

6 TEASPOONS = 2 TABLESPOONS = 1/8 CUP

12 TEASPOONS = 4 TABLESPOONS = 1/4 CUP

24 TEASPOONS = 8 TABLESPOONS = 1/2 CUP

36 TEASPOONS = 12 TABLESPOONS = 3/4 CUP

48 TEASPOONS = 16 TABLESPOONS = 1 CUP

METRIC TO US COOKING CONVERSIONS

OVEN TEMPERATURES

120 °C = 250 °F

160 °C = 320 °F

180° C = 350 °F

205 °C = 400 °F

220 °C = 425 °F

LIQUID MEASUREMENTS CONVERSION CHART

8 FLUID OUNCES = 1 CUP = 1/2 PINT = 1/4 QUART

16 FLUID OUNCES = 2 CUPS = 1 PINT = 1/2 QUART

32 FLUID OUNCES = 4 CUPS = 2 PINTS = 1 QUART

 = 1/4 GALLON

128 FLUID OUNCES = 16 CUPS = 8 PINTS = 4 QUARTS = 1 GALLON

BAKING IN GRAMS

1 CUP FLOUR = 140 GRAMS

1 CUP SUGAR = 150 GRAMS

1 CUP POWDERED SUGAR = 160 GRAMS

1 CUP HEAVY CREAM = 235 GRAMS

VOLUME

1 MILLILITER = 1/5 TEASPOON

5 ML = 1 TEASPOON

15 ML = 1 TABLESPOON

240 ML = 1 CUP OR 8 FLUID OUNCES

1 LITER = 34 FL. OUNCES

WEIGHT

1 GRAM = .035 OUNCES

100 GRAMS = 3.5 OUNCES

500 GRAMS = 1.1 POUNDS

1 KILOGRAM = 35 OUNCES

US TO METRIC COOKING CONVERSIONS

1/5 TSP = 1 ML

1 TSP = 5 ML

1 TBSP = 15 ML

1 FL OUNCE = 30 ML

1 CUP = 237 ML

1 PINT (2 CUPS) = 473 ML

1 QUART (4 CUPS) = .95 LITER

1 GALLON (16 CUPS) = 3.8 LITERS

1 OZ = 28 GRAMS

1 POUND = 454 GRAMS

BUTTER

1 CUP BUTTER = 2 STICKS = 8 OUNCES = 230 GRAMS = 8 TABLESPOONS

WHAT DOES 1 CUP EQUAL

1 CUP = 8 FLUID OUNCES

1 CUP = 16 TABLESPOONS

1 CUP = 48 TEASPOONS

1 CUP = 1/2 PINT

1 CUP = 1/4 QUART

1 CUP = 1/16 GALLON

1 CUP = 240 ML

BAKING PAN CONVERSIONS

1 CUP ALL-PURPOSE FLOUR = 4.5 OZ

1 CUP ROLLED OATS = 3 OZ 1 LARGE EGG = 1.7 OZ

1 CUP BUTTER = 8 OZ 1 CUP MILK = 8 OZ

1 CUP HEAVY CREAM = 8.4 OZ

1 CUP GRANULATED SUGAR = 7.1 OZ

1 CUP PACKED BROWN SUGAR = 7.75 OZ

1 CUP VEGETABLE OIL = 7.7 OZ

1 CUP UNSIFTED POWDERED SUGAR = 4.4 OZ

BAKING PAN CONVERSIONS

9-INCH ROUND CAKE PAN = 12 CUPS

10-INCH TUBE PAN = 16 CUPS

11-INCH BUNDT PAN = 12 CUPS

9-INCH SPRINGFORM PAN = 10 CUPS

9 X 5 INCH LOAF PAN = 8 CUPS

9-INCH SQUARE PAN = 8 CUPS

Breakfast

Pancakes

Servings: 4
Cooking Time: 29 Minutes
Ingredients:

- 1 1/2 cup coconut flour
- 1 teaspoon salt
- 3 1/2 teaspoons baking powder
- 1 tablespoon erythritol sweetener
- 1 1/2 teaspoon baking soda
- 3 tablespoons melted butter
- 1 1/4 cups milk, unsweetened, reduced-fat
- 1 egg, pastured

Directions:

1. Switch on the air fryer, insert fryer pan, grease it with olive oil, then shut with its lid, set the fryer at 220 degrees F and preheat for 5 minutes.

2. Meanwhile, take a medium bowl, add all the ingredients in it, whisk until well blended and then let the mixture rest for 5 minutes.

3. Open the fryer, pour in some of the pancake mixture as thin as possible, close with its lid and cook for 6 minutes until nicely golden, turning the pancake halfway through the frying.

4. When air fryer beeps, open its lid, transfer pancake onto a serving plate and use the remaining batter for cooking more pancakes in the same manner.

5. Serve straight away with fresh fruits slices.

Nutrition Info:

- InfoCalories: 237.7 CalCarbs: 39.2 gFat: 10.2 gProtein: 6.3 gFiber: 1.3 g

Cream Buns With Strawberries

Servings: 6
Cooking Time: 12 Minutes
Ingredients:

- 240g all-purpose flour
- 50g granulated sugar
- 8g baking powder
- 1g of salt
- 85g chopped cold butter
- 84g chopped fresh strawberries
- 120 ml whipping cream
- 2 large eggs
- 10 ml vanilla extract
- 5 ml of water

Directions:

1. Sift flour, sugar, baking powder and salt in a large bowl. Put the butter with the flour using a blender or your hands until the mixture resembles thick crumbs.

2. Mix the strawberries in the flour mixture. Set aside for the mixture to stand. Beat the whipping cream, 1 egg and the vanilla extract in a separate bowl.

3. Put the cream mixture in the flour mixture until they are homogeneous, then spread the mixture to a thickness of 38 mm.

4. Use a round cookie cutter to cut the buns. Spread the buns with a combination of egg and water. Set aside

5. Preheat the air fryer, set it to 180°C.

6. Place baking paper in the preheated inner basket.

7. Place the buns on top of the baking paper and cook for 12 minutes at 180°C, until golden brown.

Nutrition Info:

- InfoCalories: 150Fat: 14g Carbohydrates: 3g Protein: 11g Sugar: 8g Cholesterol: 0mg

Misto Quente

Servings: 4

Cooking Time: 10 Minutes

Ingredients:

- 4 slices of bread without shell
- 4 slices of turkey breast
- 4 slices of cheese
- 2 tbsp. cream cheese
- 2 spoons of butter

Directions:

1. Preheat the air fryer. Set the timer of 5 minutes and the temperature to 200C.
2. Pass the butter on one side of the slice of bread, and on the other side of the slice, the cream cheese.
3. Mount the sandwiches placing two slices of turkey breast and two slices cheese between the breads, with the cream cheese inside and the side with butter.
4. Place the sandwiches in the basket of the air fryer. Set the timer of the air fryer for 5 minutes and press the power button.

Nutrition Info:

- InfoCalories: 340 Fat: 15g Carbohydrates: 32g Protein: 15g Sugar: 0g Cholesterol: 0mg

Cauliflower Hash Browns

Servings: 6

Cooking Time: 25 Minutes

Ingredients:

- 1/4 cup chickpea flour
- 4 cups cauliflower rice
- 1/2 medium white onion, peeled and chopped
- 1/2 teaspoon garlic powder
- 1 tablespoon xanthan gum
- 1/2 teaspoon salt
- 1 tablespoon nutritional yeast flakes
- 1 teaspoon ground paprika

Directions:

1. Switch on the air fryer, insert fryer basket, grease it with olive oil, then shut with its lid, set the fryer at 375 degrees F and preheat for 10 minutes.
2. Meanwhile, place all the ingredients in a bowl, stir until well mixed and then shape the mixture into six rectangular disks, each about ½-inch thick.
3. Open the fryer, add hash browns in it in a single layer, close with its lid and cook for 25 minutes at the 375 degrees F until nicely golden and crispy, turning halfway through the frying.
4. When air fryer beeps, open its lid, transfer hash browns to a serving plate and serve.

Nutrition Info:

- InfoCalories: 115.2 CalCarbs: 6.2 gFat: 7.3 gProtein: 7.4 gFiber: 2.2 g

Grilled Cheese

Servings: 2

Cooking Time: 7 Minutes

Ingredients:

- 4 slices brown bread
- 1/2 cup shredded sharp cheddar cheese
- 1/4 cup melted butter

Directions:

1. Adjust your air fryer to 360°F.
2. In separate bowls, place cheese and butter.
3. Melt butter and brush it onto the 4 slices of bread.
4. Place cheese on 2 sides of bread slices.
5. Put sandwiches together and place them into the cooking basket.
6. Cook for 5 minutes and serve warm.

Nutrition Info:

- Info Calories: 214 kcal Total Fat: 11.2g Carbs: 9.4g Protein: 13.2g

Scotch Eggs

Servings: 4

Cooking Time: 15 Minutes

Ingredients:

- 1-pound pork sausage, pastured
- 2 tablespoons chopped parsley
- 1/8 teaspoon salt
- 1/8 teaspoon grated nutmeg
- 1 tablespoon chopped chives
- 1/8 teaspoon ground black pepper
- 2 teaspoons ground mustard, and more as needed
- 4 eggs, hard-boiled, shell peeled
- 1 cup shredded parmesan cheese, low-fat

Directions:

1. Switch on the air fryer, insert fryer basket, grease it with olive oil, then shut with its lid, set the fryer at 400 degrees F and preheat for 10 minutes.

2. Meanwhile, place sausage in a bowl, add salt, black pepper, parsley, chives, nutmeg, and mustard, then stir until well mixed and shape the mixture into four patties.

3. Peel each boiled egg, then place an egg on a patty and shape the meat around it until the egg has evenly covered.

4. Place cheese in a shallow dish, and then roll the egg in the cheese until covered completely with cheese; prepare remaining eggs in the same manner.

5. Then open the fryer, add eggs in it, close with its lid and cook for 15 minutes at the 400 degrees F until nicely golden and crispy, turning the eggs and spraying with oil halfway through the frying.

6. When air fryer beeps, open its lid, transfer eggs onto a serving plate and serve with mustard.

Nutrition Info:

- InfoCalories: 533 CalCarbs: 2 gFat: 43 gProtein: 33 gFiber: 1 g

Zucchini Bread

Servings: 8
Cooking Time: 40 Minutes
Ingredients:

- ¾ cup shredded zucchini
- 1/2 cup almond flour
- 1/4 teaspoon salt
- 1/4 cup cocoa powder, unsweetened
- 1/2 cup chocolate chips, unsweetened, divided
- 6 tablespoons erythritol sweetener
- 1/2 teaspoon baking soda
- 2 tablespoons olive oil
- 1/2 teaspoon vanilla extract, unsweetened
- 2 tablespoons butter, unsalted, melted
- 1 egg, pastured

Directions:

1. Switch on the air fryer, insert fryer basket, grease it with olive oil, then shut with its lid, set the fryer at 310 degrees F and preheat for 10 minutes.
2. Meanwhile, place flour in a bowl, add salt, cocoa powder, and baking soda and stir until mixed.
3. Crack the eggs in another bowl, whisk in sweetener, egg, oil, butter, and vanilla until smooth and then slowly whisk in flour mixture until incorporated.
4. Add zucchini along with 1/3 cup chocolate chips and then fold until just mixed.
5. Take a mini loaf pan that fits into the air fryer, grease it with olive oil, then pour in the prepared batter and sprinkle remaining chocolate chips on top.
6. Open the fryer, place the loaf pan in it, close with its lid and cook for 30 minutes at the 310 degrees F until inserted toothpick into the bread slides out clean.
7. When air fryer beeps, open its lid, remove the loaf pan, then place it on a wire rack and let the bread cool in it for 20 minutes.
8. Take out the bread, let it cool completely, then cut it into slices and serve.

Nutrition Info:

- InfoCalories: 356 CalCarbs: 49 gFat: 17 gProtein: 5.1 gFiber: 2.5 g

Tofu Scramble

Servings: 3
Cooking Time: 18 Minutes
Ingredients:

- 12 ounces tofu, extra-firm, drained, ½-inch cubed
- 1 teaspoon garlic powder
- 1 teaspoon onion powder
- 1 teaspoon paprika
- 1/2 teaspoon ground black pepper
- 1/2 teaspoon salt
- 1 tablespoon olive oil
- 2 teaspoon xanthan gum

Directions:

1. Switch on the air fryer, insert fryer basket, grease it with olive oil, then shut with its lid, set the fryer at 220 degrees F and preheat for 5 minutes.
2. Meanwhile, place tofu pieces in a bowl, drizzle with oil, and sprinkle with xanthan gum and toss until well coated.
3. Add remaining ingredients to the tofu and then toss until well coated.
4. Open the fryer, add tofu in it, close with its lid and cook for 13 minutes until nicely golden and crispy, shaking the basket every 5 minutes.
5. When air fryer beeps, open its lid, transfer tofu onto a serving plate and serve.

Nutrition Info:

- InfoCalories: 94 CalCarbs: 5 gFat: 5 gProtein: 6 gFiber: 0 g

Blueberry Buns

Servings: 6
Cooking Time: 12 Minutes
Ingredients:

- 240g all-purpose flour
- 50g granulated sugar
- 8g baking powder
- 2g of salt
- 85g chopped cold butter
- 85g of fresh blueberries
- 3g grated fresh ginger
- 113 ml whipping cream
- 2 large eggs
- 4 ml vanilla extract
- 5 ml of water

Directions:

1. Put sugar, flour, baking powder and salt in a large bowl.
2. Put the butter with the flour using a blender or your hands until the mixture resembles thick crumbs.
3. Mix the blueberries and ginger in the flour mixture and set aside
4. Mix the whipping cream, 1 egg and the vanilla extract in a different container.
5. Put the cream mixture with the flour mixture until combined.
6. Shape the dough until it reaches a thickness of approximately 38 mm and cut it into eighths.
7. Spread the buns with a combination of egg and water. Set aside Preheat the air fryer set it to 180°C.
8. Place baking paper in the preheated inner basket and place the buns on top of the paper. Cook for 12 minutes at 180°C, until golden brown

Nutrition Info:

- InfoCalories: 105 Fat: 1.64g Carbohydrates: 20.09gProtein: 2.43g Sugar: 2.1g Cholesterol: 0mg

Blueberry Muffins

Servings: 14
Cooking Time: 30 Minutes
Ingredients:

- 1 cup almond flour
- 1 cup frozen blueberries
- 2 teaspoons baking powder
- 1/3 cup erythritol sweetener
- 1 teaspoon vanilla extract, unsweetened
- ½ teaspoon salt
- ¼ cup melted coconut oil
- 1 egg, pastured
- ¼ cup applesauce, unsweetened
- ¼ cup almond milk, unsweetened

Directions:

1. Switch on the air fryer, insert fryer basket, grease it with olive oil, then shut with its lid, set the fryer at 360 degrees F and preheat for 10 minutes.
2. Meanwhile, place flour in a large bowl, add berries, salt, sweetener, and baking powder and stir until well combined.
3. Crack the eggs in another bowl, whisk in vanilla, milk, and applesauce until combined and then slowly whisk in flour mixture until incorporated.
4. Take fourteen silicone muffin cups, grease them with oil, and then evenly fill them with the prepared batter.
5. Open the fryer, stack muffin cups in it, close with its lid and cook for 10 minutes until muffins are nicely golden brown and set.
6. When air fryer beeps, open its lid, transfer muffins onto a serving plate and then remaining muffins in the same manner.
7. Serve straight away.

Nutrition Info:

- InfoCalories: 201 CalCarbs: 27.3 gFat: 8.8 gProtein: 3 gFiber: 1.2 g

Bacon Bbq

Servings: 2

Cooking Time: 8 Minutes

Ingredients:

- 13g dark brown sugar
- 5g chili powder
- 1g ground cumin
- 1g cayenne pepper
- 4 slices bacon, halved

Directions:

1. Mix seasonings until well combined.
2. Dip the bacon in the dressing until it is completely covered. Leave aside.
3. Adjust the air fryer to 160°C.
4. Place the bacon in the preheated air fryer
5. Select Bacon option and press Start/Pause. Serve.

Nutrition Info:

- Info Calories: 1124 kcal Fat: 72g Carbs: 59g Protein: 49g

Cocotte Eggs

Servings: 1

Cooking Time: 15 Minutes

Ingredients:

- 1 tbsp. olive oil soup
- 2 tbsp. crumbly ricotta
- 1 tbsp. parmesan cheese soup
- 1 slice of gorgonzola cheese
- 1 slice of Brie cheese
- 1 tbsp. cream soup
- 1 egg
- Nutmeg and salt to taste
- Butternut to taste

Directions:

1. Spread with olive oil in the bottom of a small glass refractory. Place the cheese in the bottom and season with nutmeg and salt. Add the cream.
2. Break the egg into a cup and gently add it to the refractory mixture.
3. Preheat the air fryer for the time of 5 minutes and the temperature at 200C. Put the refractory in the basket of the air fryer, set the time to 10 minutes, and press the power button. Remove and serve still hot.

Nutrition Info:

- Info Calories: 138 Cal Carbs: 3 g Fat: 33 g Protein: 7.4 g Fiber: 2.2 g

Broccoli Mash

Servings: 4

Cooking Time: 20-30 Minutes

Ingredients:

- 20 oz. Broccoli florets
- 3 oz. Butter; melted
- 1 garlic clove; minced
- 4 tbsp. Basil; chopped.
- A drizzle of olive oil
- A pinch of salt and black pepper

Directions:

1. Take a bowl and mix the broccoli with the oil, salt and pepper, toss and transfer to your air fryer's basket.
2. Cook at 380°f for 20 minutes, cool the broccoli down and put it in a blender
3. Add the rest of the ingredients, pulse, divide the mash between plates and serve as a side dish.

Nutrition Info:

- Info Calories: 200 Fat: 14g Fiber: 3g Carbs: 6g Protein: 7g

French Toast In Sticks

Servings: 4

Cooking Time: 10 Minutes

Ingredients:

- 4 slices of white bread, 38 mm thick, preferably hard
- 2 eggs
- 60 ml of milk
- 15 ml maple sauce
- 2 ml vanilla extract
- Nonstick Spray Oil
- 38g of sugar
- 3ground cinnamon
- Maple syrup, to serve
- Sugar to sprinkle

Directions:

1. Cut each slice of bread into thirds making 12 pieces. Place sideways
2. Beat the eggs, milk, maple syrup and vanilla.
3. Preheat the air fryer, set it to 175°C.
4. Dip the sliced   bread in the egg mixture and place it in the preheated air fryer. Sprinkle French toast generously with oil spray.
5. Cook French toast for 10 minutes at 175°C. Turn the toast halfway through cooking.
6. Mix the sugar and cinnamon in a bowl.
7. Cover the French toast with the sugar and cinnamon mixture when you have finished cooking.
8. Serve with Maple syrup and sprinkle with powdered sugar

Nutrition Info:

- Info Calories 128 Fat 6.2 g, Carbohydrates 16.3 g, Sugar 3.3 g, Protein 3.2 g, Cholesterol 17 mg

Breakfast Pizza

Servings: 1-2
Cooking Time: 8 Minutes
Ingredients:
- 10 ml of olive oil
- 1 prefabricated pizza dough (178 mm)
- 28g low moisture mozzarella cheese
- 2 slices smoked ham
- 1 egg
- 2g chopped cilantro

Directions:
1. Pass olive oil over the prefabricated pizza dough.
2. Add mozzarella cheese and smoked ham in the dough.
3. Preheat the air fryer, set it to 175°C.
4. Place the pizza in the preheated air fryer and cook for 8 minutes at 175°C.
5. Remove the baskets after 5 minutes and open the egg on the pizza.
6. Replace the baskets in the air fryer and finish cooking. Garnish with chopped coriander and serve.

Nutrition Info:
- InfoCalories: 224 Fat: 7.5g Carbohydrates: 25.2g Protein: 14g Sugar: 0g Cholesterol: 13mg

Garlic Bread

Servings: 5
Cooking Time: 15 Minutes
Ingredients:
- 2 stale French rolls
- 4 tbsps. Crushed or crumpled garlic
- 1 cup mayonnaise
- Powdered grated Parmesan
- 1 tbsp. olive oil

Directions:
1. Preheat the air fryer to 200°C for 5 minutes.
2. Mix mayonnaise with garlic and set aside.
3. Cut the baguettes into slices, but without separating them completely.
4. Fill the cavities of equals, then brush with olive oil and sprinkle with grated cheese.
5. Place in the basket of the air fryer. Cook for 10 minutes at 180°C. Serve.

Nutrition Info:
- Info Calories: 151 kcal Fat: 7.1g Carbs: 17.9g Protein: 3.6g

Zucchini And Walnut Cake With Maple Flavor Icing

Servings: 5

Cooking Time: 35 Minutes

Ingredients:

- 1 9-ounce package of yellow cake mix
- 1 egg
- ⅓ cup of water
- ½ cup grated zucchini
- ¼ cup chopped walnuts
- ¾ tsp. of cinnamon
- ¼ tsp. nutmeg
- ¼ tsp. ground ginger
- Maple Flavor Glaze

Directions:

1. Preheat the fryer to a temperature of 350°F. Prepare an 8 x 3⅞ inch loaf pan. Prepare the cake dough according to package directions, using ⅓ cup of water instead of ½ cup. Add zucchini, nuts, cinnamon, nutmeg, and ginger.

2. Pour the dough into the prepared mold and put it inside the basket. Bake until a toothpick inserted in the middle of the cake is clean when removed for 32 to 34 minutes.

3. Remove the cake from the fryer and let it cool on a grill for 10 minutes. Then, remove the cake and place it on a serving plate. Stop cooling just warm. Spray it with maple flavor glaze.

Nutrition Info:

- InfoCalories: 196 Carbohydrates: 27gFat: 11g Protein: 1g Sugar: 7g Cholesterol: 0mg

Scallion Sandwich

Servings: 1

Cooking Time: 15 Minutes

Ingredients:

- 2 slices wheat bread
- 2 tsps. Low-fat butter
- 2 sliced scallions
- 1 tbsp. grated parmesan cheese
- 3/4 cup low-fat, grated cheddar cheese

Directions:

1. Adjust the Air fryer to 356ºF.
2. Apply butter to a slice of bread.
3. Then place it inside the cooking air fryer basket with the butter side facing down.
4. Place cheese and scallions on top. Spread the rest of the butter on the other slice of bread. Then put it on top of the sandwich.
5. Allow to cook for 10 minutes. Serve.

Nutrition Info:

- Info Calories: 154 kcal Carbs: 9g Fat: 2.5g Protein: 8.6g

Tortilla

Servings: Two
Cooking Time: 20 Minutes
Ingredients:

- 2 eggs
- 2 slices of ham, chopped
- 2 slices of chopped mozzarella
- 1 tbsp. chopped onion soup
- ½ cup chopped parsley and chives tea
- Salt, black pepper and oregano to taste
- Olive oil spread

Directions:

1. Preheat the air fryer for the time of 5 minutes and the temperature at 200C.
2. Spread a refractory that fits in the basket of the air fryer and has a high shelf and reserve.
3. In a bowl, beat the eggs lightly with a fork. Add the fillings and spices. Place the refractory container in the basket of the air fryer and pour the beaten eggs being careful not to fall.
4. Set the time from 10 to 15 minutes and press the power button. The tortilla is ready when it is golden brown

Nutrition Info:

- InfoCalories: 41 Fat: 1.01g Carbohydrates: 6.68g Protein: 1.08g Sugar: 0.25g Cholesterol: 0mg

Herb Frittata

Servings: 4
Cooking Time: 25 Minutes
Ingredients:

- 2 tablespoons chopped green scallions
- 1/2 teaspoon ground black pepper
- 2 tablespoons chopped cilantro
- 1/2 teaspoon salt
- 2 tablespoons chopped parsley
- 1/2 cup half and half, reduced-fat
- 4 eggs, pastured
- 1/3 cup shredded cheddar cheese, reduced-fat

Directions:

1. Switch on the air fryer, insert fryer basket, grease it with olive oil, then shut with its lid, set the fryer at 330 degrees F and preheat for 10 minutes.
2. Meanwhile, take a round heatproof pan that fits into the fryer basket, grease it well with oil and set aside until required.
3. Crack the eggs in a bowl, beat in half-and-half, then add remaining ingredients, beat until well mixed and pour the mixture into prepared pan.
4. Open the fryer, place the pan in it, close with its lid and cook for 15 minutes at the 330 degrees F until its top is nicely golden, frittata has set and inserted toothpick into the frittata slides out clean.
5. When air fryer beeps, open its lid, take out the pan, then transfer frittata onto a serving plate, cut it into pieces and serve.

Nutrition Info:

- InfoCalories: 141 CalCarbs: 2 gFat: 10 gProtein: 8 gFiber: 0 g

Lean Lamb And Turkey Meatballs With Yogurt

Servings: 4

Cooking Time:x

Ingredients:

- 1 egg white
- 4 ounces ground lean turkey
- 1 pound of ground lean lamb
- 1 teaspoon each of cayenne pepper, ground coriander, red chili paste, salt, and ground cumin
- 2 garlic cloves, minced
- 1 1/2 tablespoons parsley, chopped
- 1 tablespoon mint, chopped
- 1/4 cup of olive oil
- For the yogurt
- 2 tablespoons of buttermilk
- 1 garlic clove, minced
- 1/4 cup mint, chopped
- 1/2 cup of Greek yogurt, non-fat
- Salt to taste

Directions:

1. Set the Air Fryer to 390 degrees.
2. Mix all the ingredients for the meatballs in a bowl. Roll and mold them into golf-size round pieces. Arrange in the cooking basket. Cook for 8 minutes.
3. While waiting, combine all the ingredients for the mint yogurt in a bowl. Mix well.
4. Serve the meatballs with the mint yogurt. Top with olives and fresh mint.

Nutrition Info:

- Info Calorie: 154 Carbohydrate: 9g Fat: 2.5g Protein: 8.6g Fiber: 2.4g

Chickpea, Tuna, And Kale Salad

Servings: 1

Cooking Time: None

Ingredients:

- 2 ounces fresh kale
- 2 tablespoons fat-free honey mustard dressing
- 1 (3-ounce) pouch tuna in water, drained
- 1 medium carrot, shredded
- Salt and pepper

Directions:

1. Trim the thick stems from the kale and cut into bite-sized pieces.
2. Toss the kale with the dressing in a salad bowl.
3. Top with tuna, chickpeas, and carrots. Season with salt and pepper to serve.

Nutrition Info:

- Info Calories 215Total Fat 0.6g Saturated Fat 0g Total Carbs 28.1g Net Carbs 23.6g Protein 22.5g Sugar 16g Fiber 4.5g Sodium 1176mg

Appetizers And Siders

Vegan Breakfast Sandwich

Servings: 4
Cooking Time: 10 Minutes
Ingredients:

- Tofu (Egg)
- Garlic powder: 1 teaspoon
- Light soy sauce: 1/4 cup
- Turmeric: 1/2 teaspoon
- 1 block extra firm pressed tofu: cut into 4 round slices
- Breakfast Sandwich
- English muffins: four pieces, vegan
- Avocado: one cut into slices
- Tomato slices
- Vegan cheese: 4 slices
- Sliced onions
- Vegan mayonnaise or vegan butter

Directions:

1. Let the tofu marinate overnight.
2. In a deep dish, add the tofu circles with turmeric, soy sauce, and garlic powder. Let it for 10 minutes or overnight.
3. Put the tofu (marinated) in an air fryer. Cook for ten minutes at 400 F. shake the basket after 5 minutes.
4. Add vegan butter or vegan mayonnaise to the English muffins. Add vegan cheese, avocado slices, tomato, onions slices, and marinated, cooked tofu. Top with the other half of the English muffin.
5. Serve right away and enjoy.

Nutrition Info:

- Info Cal 198|fat 10 g| carbs 12 g| protein 19.9 g

Air Fryer Bacon-wrapped Jalapeno Poppers

Servings: 10
Cooking Time: 8 Minutes
Ingredients:

- Cream cheese: 1/3 cup
- Ten jalapenos
- Thin bacon: 5 strips

Directions:

1. Wash and pat dry the jalapenos. Cut them in half and take out the seeds.
2. Add the cream cheese in the middle, but do not put too much
3. Let the air fryer preheat to 370 F. cut the bacon strips in half.
4. Wrap the cream cheese filled jalapenos with slices of bacon.
5. Secure with a toothpick.
6. Place the wrapped jalapenos in an air fryer, cook at 370 F and cook for 6-8 minutes or until the bacon is crispy.
7. Serve hot.

Nutrition Info:

- Info Calories: 76kcal | Carbohydrates: 1g | Protein: 2g | Fat: 7g |

Easy Air Fryer Omelet

Servings: 2

Cooking Time: 15 Minutes

Ingredients:

- Breakfast Seasoning: 1 teaspoon
- Two eggs
- A pinch of salt
- Fresh ham
- Milk: 1/4 cup
- Shredded cheese: 1/4 cup
- Diced veggies: green onions, red bell pepper, and mushrooms

Directions:

1. In a bowl, mix the milk and eggs, combine them well. Season with a pinch of salt.
2. Add the chopped vegetables to the egg mixture.
3. Add the egg mixture to a 6"x3" baking pan. Make sure it is well greased.
4. Put the pan in the air fryer basket.
5. Air fry for 8-10 minutes at 350° Fahrenheit.
6. After 5 minutes, add the breakfast seasoning into the eggs and top with shredded cheese.
7. Take out from the air fryer, and transfer to the plate.
8. Serve hot with extra green onions and enjoy.

Nutrition Info:

- Info Cal 256| fat 13 g| protein 15 g| carbs 8 g

Avocado Fries

Servings: 2

Cooking Time: 20 Minutes

Ingredients:

- 1 medium avocado, pitted
- 1 egg
- 1/2 cup almond flour
- ¼ teaspoon salt
- ¼ teaspoon ground black pepper
- 1/2 teaspoon salt

Directions:

1. Switch on the air fryer, insert fryer basket, grease it with olive oil, then shut with its lid, set the fryer at 400 degrees F and preheat for 10 minutes.
2. Meanwhile, cut the avocado in half and then cut each half into wedges, each about ½-inch thick.
3. Place flour in a shallow dish, add salt and black pepper and stir until mixed.
4. Crack the egg in a bowl and then whisk until blended.
5. Working on one avocado piece at a time, first dip it in the egg, then coat it in the almond flour mixture and place it on a wire rack.
6. Open the fryer, add avocado pieces in it in a single layer, spray oil over avocado, close with its lid and cook for 10 minutes until nicely golden and crispy, shaking halfway through the frying.
7. When air fryer beeps, open its lid, transfer avocado fries onto a serving plate and serve.

Nutrition Info:

- InfoCalories: 251 CalCarbs: 19 gFat: 17 gProtein: 6 gFiber: 7 g

Pork Sticks

Servings: 2
Cooking Time: 15 Minutes
Ingredients:

- 1 lb. boneless pork
- 2 cup dry breadcrumbs
- 2 tsp. oregano
- 2- tsp. red chili flakes
- Marinade:
- 1 ½- tbsp. ginger-garlic paste
- 4- tbsp. lemon juice
- 2- tsp. salt
- 1 tsp. pepper powder
- 1 tsp. red chili powder
- 6- tbsp. corn flour
- 4- eggs

Directions:

1. Blend all marinade ingredients and soak the meat for 20-30 minutes.
2. Blend the breadcrumbs, oregano and red chili well and dip the marinated fingers in this mix.
3. Preheat the Air Fryer to 160 F for 5 minutes.
4. Cook for 15 minutes, shaking halfway through.

Nutrition Info:

- Info Calories 725 Fat 57 g Carbohydrates 4 g Sugar 0.7 g Protein 49 g Cholesterol 108 mg

Parmesan Zucchini Rounds

Servings: 4
Cooking Time: 20 Minutes
Ingredients:

- 4 zucchinis; sliced
- 1 ½ cups parmesan; grated
- ¼ cup parsley; chopped.
- 1 egg; whisked
- 1 egg white; whisked
- ½ tsp. garlic powder
- Cooking spray

Directions:

1. Get a bowl and mix the egg with egg whites, parmesan, parsley and garlic powder and whisk.
2. Dredge each zucchini slice in this mix, place them all in your air fryer's basket, grease them with cooking spray and cook at 370°F for 20 minutes
3. Divide between plates and serve as a side dish.

Nutrition Info:

- Info Calories: 183 Fat: 6g Fiber: 2g Carbs: 3g Protein: 8g

Air Fryer Mini Pizza

Servings: 1

Cooking Time:5 Minutes

Ingredients:

- Sliced olives: 1/4 cup
- One pita bread
- One tomato
- Shredded cheese: 1/2 cup

Directions:

1. Let the air fryer preheat to 350 F
2. Lay pita flat on a plate. Add cheese, slices of tomatoes, and olives.
3. Cook for five minutes at 350 F
4. Take the pizza out of the air fryer.
5. Slice it and enjoy

Nutrition Info:

- Info Calories: 344kcal | Carbohydrates: 37g | Protein: 18g | Fat: 13g |

Keto French Fries

Servings: 4

Cooking Time: 20 Minutes

Ingredients:

- 1 large rutabaga, peeled and cut into spears about ¼ inch wide.
- Salt and pepper
- 1/2 tsp. paprika
- 2 tbsps. coconut oil

Directions:

1. Preheat your air fryer to 450°F.
2. Mix the oil, paprika, salt, and pepper.
3. Pour the oil mixture over the fries, making sure all pieces are well coated.
4. Cook in the air fryer for 20 minutes or until crispy.

Nutrition Info:

- Info Calories: 113 kcal; Fat: 7.2g; Carbs: 12.5g; Protein: 1.9g

Air Fryer Buffalo Cauliflower

Servings: 4

Cooking Time:15 Minutes

Ingredients:

- Homemade buffalo sauce: 1/2 cup
- One head of cauliflower, cut bite-size pieces
- Butter melted: 1 tablespoon
- Olive oil
- Kosher salt & pepper, to taste

Directions:

1. Spray cooking oil on the air fryer basket.
2. In a bowl, add buffalo sauce, melted butter, pepper, and salt. Mix well.
3. Put the cauliflower bits in the air fryer and spray the olive oil over it. Let it cook at 400 F for 7 minutes.
4. Remove the cauliflower from the air fryer and add it to the sauce. Coat the cauliflower well.
5. Put the sauce coated cauliflower back into the air fryer.
6. Cook at 400 F, for 7-8 minutes or until crispy.
7. Take out from the air fryer and serve with dipping sauce.

Nutrition Info:

- Info Calories 101kcal | Carbohydrates 4g | Protein 3g | Fat: 7g

Chicken Croquette

Servings: 4

Cooking Time: 15 Minutes

Ingredients:

- 2- lb. boneless chicken
- 1st Marinade:
- 3- tbsp. vinegar or lemon juice
- 2 or 3 tsp. paprika
- 1 tsp. black pepper
- 1 tsp. salt
- 3 tsp. ginger-garlic paste
- 2nd Marinade:
- 1 cup yogurt
- 4- tsp. tandoori masala
- 2- tbsp. dry fenugreek leaves
- 1 tsp. black salt
- 1 tsp. chat masala
- 1 tsp. garam masala powder
- 1 tsp. red chili powder
- 1 tsp. salt
- 3- drops of red color

Directions:

1. Make the 1st marinade and drench the chicken in it for 4 hours.
2. Make the 2nd marinade and sprinkle the chicken in it to let the flavors blend.
3. Preheat the Air Fryer to 160 F and cook for 15 minutes.
4. Serve with mint chutney.

Nutrition Info:

- Info Calories: 73 Protein: 1.1g Fiber: 1.1g Fat: 6.5g Carbs: 3.3g

Roasted Chickpeas

Servings: 6

Cooking Time: 25 Minutes

Ingredients:

- 15-ounce cooked chickpeas
- 1 teaspoon garlic powder
- 1 tablespoon nutritional yeast
- 1/8 teaspoon cumin
- 1 teaspoon smoked paprika
- 1/2 teaspoon salt
- 1 tablespoon olive oil

Directions:

1. Take a large baking sheet, line it with paper towels, then spread chickpeas on it, cover the peas with paper towels, and let rest for 30 minutes or until chickpeas are dried.
2. Then switch on the air fryer, insert fryer basket, grease it with olive oil, then shut with its lid, set the fryer at 355 degrees F and preheat for 5 minutes.
3. Place dried chickpeas in a bowl, add remaining ingredients and toss until well coated.
4. Open the fryer, add chickpeas in it, close with its lid and cook for 20 minutes until nicely golden and crispy, shaking the chickpeas every 5 minutes.
5. When air fryer beeps, open its lid, transfer chickpeas onto a serving bowl and serve.

Nutrition Info:

- InfoCalories: 124 CalCarbs: 17.4 gFat: 4.4 gProtein: 4.7 gFiber: 4 g

Spinach And Artichokes Sauté

Servings: 4

Cooking Time: 15 Minutes

Ingredients:

- 10 oz. artichoke hearts; halved
- 2 cups baby spinach
- 3 garlic cloves
- ¼ cup veggie stock
- 2 tsp. lime juice
- Salt and black pepper to taste.

Directions:

1. In a pan that fits your air fryer, mix all the ingredients, toss, introduce in the fryer and cook at 370°F for 15 minutes
2. Divide between plates and serve as a side dish.

Nutrition Info:

- Info Calories: 209 Fat: 6g Fiber: 2g Carbs: 4g Protein: 8g

Veal Chili

Servings: 4

Cooking Time: 15 Minutes

Ingredients:

- 1 lb. veal
- 2 ½- tsp. ginger-garlic paste
- 1 tsp. red chili sauce
- ¼- tsp. salt
- ¼- tsp. red chili powder/black pepper
- Edible orange food coloring
- For sauce:
- 2- tbsp. olive oil
- 1 ½- tsp. ginger garlic paste
- ½- tbsp. red chili sauce
- 2 -tbsp. tomato ketchup
- 2- tsp. soy sauce
- 1-2 tbsp. honey
- ¼- tsp. Ajinomoto
- 1-2 tsp. red chili flakes

Directions:

1. Blend all of the components for the marinade and marinate veal fingers for 30 minutes.
2. Blend the breadcrumbs, oregano and red chili flakes and add the marinated fingers on this mix.
3. Preheat the Air Fryer to 160 F and cook for 15 minutes, shaking the fry basket occasionally.

Nutrition Info:

- Info Calories: 121 Protein: 9.9g Fiber: 0.6g Fat: 6.7g Carbs: 3.8g

Roasted Eggplant

Servings: 4
Cooking Time: 30 Minutes
Ingredients:

- 1 large eggplant
- tbsps. Olive oil
- 1/2 tsp. Garlic powder.
- Salt

Directions:

1. Remove top and bottom from the eggplant. Slice eggplant into 1/4-inch-thick round slices.
2. Brush slices with olive oil. Sprinkle with salt and garlic powder
3. Place eggplant slices into the air fryer basket. Adjust the temperature to 390°F and set the timer for 15 minutes. Serve immediately.

Nutrition Info:

- Info Calories: 91 kcal; Protein: 1.3g; Fat: 6.7g; Carbs: 7.5g

Salmon Tandoor

Servings: 3
Cooking Time: 15 Minutes
Ingredients:

- 2 lb. boneless salmon filets
- 1st Marinade:
- 3 tbsp. vinegar or lemon juice
- 2 or 3 tsp. paprika
- 1 tsp. black pepper
- 1 tsp. salt
- 3 tsp. ginger-garlic paste
- 2nd Marinade:
- 1 cup yogurt
- 4- tsp. tandoori masala
- 2- tbsp. dry fenugreek leaves
- 1 tsp. black salt
- 1 tsp. chat masala
- 1 tsp. garam masala powder
- 1 tsp. red chili powder
- 1 tsp. salt
- 3- drops of red color

Directions:

1. Make the 1st marinade and drench the salmon in it for 4 hours.
2. Make the 2nd marinade and sprinkle the salmon in it to let the flavors blend.
3. Preheat the Air Fryer to 160 F and cook for 15 minutes.
4. Serve with mint chutney.

Nutrition Info:

- Info Calories 160 Fat 1 g Carbohydrates 1 g Sugar 0.5 g Protein 22 g Cholesterol 60 mg

Green Beans

Servings: 4

Cooking Time: 20 Minutes

Ingredients:

- 6 cups green beans; trimmed
- 1 tbsp. hot paprika
- 2 tbsp. olive oil
- A pinch of salt and black pepper

Directions:

1. Get a bowl and mix the green beans with the other ingredients, toss, put them in the air fryer's basket and cook at 370°F for 20 minutes
2. Divide between plates and serve as a side dish.

Nutrition Info:

- Info Calories: 120 Fat: 5g Fiber: 1g Carbs: 4g Protein: 2g

Chinese Chili

Servings: 4

Cooking Time: 15 Minutes

Ingredients:

- For chicken fingers:
- 1 lb. chicken
- 2 ½- tsp. ginger-garlic paste
- 1 tsp. red chili sauce
- ¼- tsp. salt
- ¼- tsp. red chili powder/black pepper
- Edible orange food coloring
- For sauce:
- 2- tbsp. olive oil
- 1 ½- tsp. ginger garlic paste
- ½- tbsp. red chili sauce
- 2- tbsp. tomato ketchup
- 2- tsp. soy sauce
- 1-2- tbsp. honey
- ¼- tsp. Ajinomoto
- 1-2- tsp. red chili flakes

Directions:

1. Blend all of the components for the marinade and marinate chicken fingers for 30 minutes.
2. Blend the breadcrumbs, oregano and red chili flakes and add the marinated fingers on this mix.
3. Preheat the Air Fryer to 160 F and cook for 15 minutes, shaking the fry basket occasionally.

Nutrition Info:

- Info Calories 545 Fat 39.6 g Carbohydrates 9.5 g Sugar 3.1 g Protein 43 g Cholesterol 110 mg

Air Fryer Spanakopita Bites

Servings: 4

Cooking Time:15 Minutes

Ingredients:

- 4 sheets phyllo dough
- Baby spinach leaves: 2 cups
- Grated Parmesan cheese: 2 tablespoons
- Low-fat cottage cheese: 1/4 cup
- Dried oregano: 1 teaspoon
- Feta cheese: 6 tbsp. crumbled
- Water: 2 tablespoons
- One egg white only
- Lemon zest: 1 teaspoon
- Cayenne pepper: 1/8 teaspoon
- Olive oil: 1 tablespoon
- Kosher salt and freshly ground black pepper: 1/4 teaspoon, each

Directions:

1. In a pot over high heat, add water and spinach, cook until wilted.

2. Drain it and cool for ten minutes. Squeeze out excess moisture.

3. In a bowl, mix cottage cheese, Parmesan cheese, oregano, salt, cayenne pepper, egg white, freshly ground black pepper, feta cheese, spinach, and zest. Mix it well or in the food processor.

4. Lay one phyllo sheet on a flat surface. Spray with oil. Add the second sheet of phyllo on top—spray oil. Add a total of 4 oiled sheets.

5. Form 16 strips from these four oiled sheets. Add one tbsp of filling in one strip. Roll it around the filling.

6. Spray the air fryer basket with oil. Put eight bites in the basket, spray with oil. Cook for 12 minutes at 375°F until crispy and golden brown. Flip halfway through.

7. Serve hot.

Nutrition Info:

- Info Calories 82|Fat 4g|Protein 4g|Carbohydrate 7g

Balsamic Cabbage

Servings: 4

Cooking Time: Minutes

Ingredients:

- 6 cups red cabbage; shredded
- 4 garlic cloves; minced
- 1 tbsp. olive oil
- 1 tbsp. balsamic vinegar
- Salt and black pepper to taste.

Directions:

1. In a pan that fits the air fryer, combine all the ingredients, toss, introduce the pan in the air fryer and cook at 380°F for 15 minutes

2. Divide between plates and serve as a side dish.

Nutrition Info:

- Info Calories: 151 Fat: 2g Fiber: 3g Carbs: 5g Protein: 5g

Nutella Smores

Servings: 4
Cooking Time: 5 Minutes
Ingredients:

- 4 Graham crackers, halved
- 2 half-cut jumbo marshmallows
- Strawberries and Raspberries
- 4 tsps. Nutella

Directions:

1. Preheat the air fryer to 350°F.
2. Place 4 graham cracker halves in the air fryer basket.
3. Put 1 marshmallow on top of each graham cracker half. Cook for 5 minutes, till marshmallow is nice and golden.
4. Add the berries and the Nutella. Top each with a graham cracker half.
5. Serve.

Nutrition Info:

- Info Calories: 401 kcal; Fat: 15g; Carbs: 61g; Protein: 4g

Air Fryer Roasted Bananas

Servings: 1
Cooking Time: 8 Minutes
Ingredients:

- 1 banana, sliced into 1/8-inch pieces
- Avocado oil

Directions:

1. Set a parchment paper to your air fryer basket.
2. Set the banana pieces on the basket and avoid overlapping. You can cook in batches if need be. Sprinkle avocado oil to the slices.
3. Set in the air fryer and allow to cook for 5 minutes at 375F. You can add 3 extra minutes to ensure they are browned and caramelized.

Nutrition Info:

- Info Calories: 107 kcal; Carbs: 27g; Proteins: 1.3g; Fat: 0.7g

Avocado Egg Rolls

Servings: 10
Cooking Time: 15 Minutes
Ingredients:

- Ten egg roll wrappers
- Diced sundried tomatoes: ¼ cup oil drained
- Avocados, cut in cube
- Red onion: 2/3 cup chopped
- 1/3 cup chopped cilantro
- Kosher salt and freshly ground black pepper
- Two small limes: juice

Directions:

1. In a bowl, add sundried tomatoes, avocado, cilantro, lime juice, pepper, onion, and kosher salt mix well gently.
2. Lay egg roll wrapper flat on a surface, add ¼ cup of filling in the wrapper's bottom.
3. Seal with water and make it into a roll.
4. Spray the rolls with olive oil.
5. Cook at 400 F in the air fryer for six minutes. Turn halfway through.
6. Serve with dipping sauce.

Nutrition Info:

- Info 160 Cal| total fat 19g |carbohydrates 5.6g |protein 19.2g

Crispy Fat-free Spanish Potatoes

Servings: 3

Cooking Time: 35 Minutes

Ingredients:

- Small red potatoes: 1 and 1/2 pounds
- Liquid from cooked chickpeas or aquafaba: 1 tablespoon
- Tomato paste: 1 teaspoon
- Sea salt optional: 1 teaspoon
- Brown rice flour or any flour (your choice): half tablespoon
- Smoked Spanish paprika: 1 teaspoon
- Garlic powder: half teaspoon
- Sweet smoked paprika: 3/4 tsp.

Directions:

1. Wash and pat dry the potatoes. Cut the potatoes into small quarters, makes sure they are the same sized. The maximum thickness of potatoes should be one and a half-inch thick.
2. Boil the potatoes wedges however you like,
3. Drain the potatoes wedges and add them in a large bowl.
4. In another bowl, add tomato paste and aquafaba. In the small bowl, mix the remaining ingredients and flour.
5. Now add the tomato paste mixture to the potatoes, coat all the potatoes wedges gently with light hands. Add the dry mix to the coated potatoes until every potato is covered.
6. Let the air fryer preheat to 360F for 3 minutes. Place the potatoes in the air fryer basket and cook for 12 minutes.
7. Shake the basket of air fryer every six minutes. Make sure no potatoes get stuck on the bottom.
8. Let the potatoes be crispy to your liking.
9. Serve hot with dipping sauce.

Nutrition Info:

- Info Calories 171|Carbohydrates 39g|Fiber 5g|Protein 5g

Onion Rings

Servings: 4

Cooking Time: 32 Minutes

Ingredients:

- 1 large white onion, peeled
- 2/3 cup pork rinds
- 3 tablespoons almond flour
- 1/2 teaspoon garlic powder
- 1/2 teaspoon paprika
- 1/4 teaspoon sea salt
- 3 tablespoons coconut flour
- 2 eggs, pastured

Directions:

1. Switch on the air fryer, insert fryer basket, grease it with olive oil, then shut with its lid, set the fryer at 400 degrees F and preheat for 10 minutes.
2. Meanwhile, slice the peeled onion into ½ inch thick rings.
3. Take a shallow dish, add almond flour and stir in garlic powder, paprika, and pork rinds; take another shallow dish, add coconut flour and salt and stir until mixed.
4. Crack eggs in a bowl and then whisk until combined.
5. Working on one onion ring at a time, first coat onion ring in coconut flour mixture, then it in egg, and coat with pork rind mixture by scooping over the onion until evenly coated.
6. Open the fryer, place coated onion rings in it in a single layer, spray oil over onion rings, close with its lid and cook for 16 minutes until nicely golden and thoroughly cooked, flipping the onion rings halfway through the frying.
7. When air fryer beeps, open its lid, transfer onion rings onto a serving plate and cook the remaining onion rings in the same manner.
8. Serve straight away.

Nutrition Info:

- InfoCalories: 135 CalCarbs: 8 gFat: 7 gProtein: 8 gFiber: 3 g

Roasted Tomatoes

Servings: 4

Cooking Time: 15 Minutes

Ingredients:

- 4 tomatoes; halved
- ½ cup parmesan; grated
- 1 tbsp. basil; chopped.
- ½ tsp. onion powder
- ½ tsp. oregano; dried
- ½ tsp. smoked paprika
- ½ tsp. garlic powder
- Cooking spray

Directions:

1. Get a bowl and mix all the ingredients except the cooking spray and the parmesan.
2. Arrange the tomatoes in your air fryer's pan, sprinkle the parmesan on top and grease with cooking spray
3. Cook at 370°F for 15 minutes, divide between plates and serve.

Nutrition Info:

- Info Calories: 200 Fat: 7g Fiber: 2g Carbs: 4g Protein: 6g

Poultry

Chicken's Liver

Servings: 4
Cooking Time: 30 Minutes
Ingredients:

- 500g of chicken livers
- 2 or 3 carrots
- 1 green pepper
- 1 red pepper
- 1 onion
- 4 tomatoes
- Salt
- Ground pepper
- 1 glass of white wine
- ½ glass of water
- Extra virgin olive oil

Directions:

1. Peel the carrots, cut them into slices and add them to the bowl of the air fryer with a tablespoon of extra virgin olive oil 5 minutes.
2. After 5 minutes, add the peppers and onion in julienne. Select 5 minutes.
3. After that time, add the tomatoes in wedges and select 5 more minutes.
4. Add now the chicken liver clean and chopped.
5. Season, add the wine and water.
6. Select 10 minutes.
7. Check that the liver is tender.

Nutrition Info:

- Info Calories: 76 Fat: 13g Carbohydrates: 1g Protein: 2Sugar: 1gCholesterol: 130mg

Herb Chicken Thighs

Servings: 6
Cooking Time: 40 Minutes
Ingredients:

- 6 chicken thighs, skin-on, pastured
- 2 teaspoons garlic powder
- 1/2 teaspoon onion powder
- 1 teaspoon dried basil
- 1 teaspoon spike seasoning
- 1/2 teaspoon dried sage
- 1/4 teaspoon ground black pepper
- 1/2 teaspoon dried oregano
- 2 tablespoons lemon juice
- 1/4 cup olive oil

Directions:

1. Prepare the marinade and for this, place all the ingredients in a bowl, except for chicken, stir until well combined and then pour the marinade in a large plastic bag.
2. Add chicken thighs in the plastic bag, seal the bag, then turn in upside down until chicken thighs are coated with the marinade and let marinate in the refrigerator for minimum of 6 hours.
3. Then drain the chicken, arrange the chicken thighs on a wire rack and let them rest for 15 minutes at room temperature.
4. Meanwhile, switch on the air fryer, insert fryer basket, grease it with olive oil, then shut with its lid, set the fryer at 360 degrees F and preheat for 5 minutes.
5. Then open the fryer, add chicken thighs in it in a single layer top-side down, close with its lid, cook the chicken for 8 minutes, turn the chicken, and continue frying for 6 minutes.
6. Turn the chicken thighs and then continue cooking for another 6 minutes or until chicken is nicely browned and cooked.
7. When air fryer beeps, open its lid, transfer chicken onto a serving plate and cook the remaining chicken thighs in the same manner.
8. Serve straight away.

Nutrition Info:

- InfoCalories: 163 CalCarbs: 1 gFat: 9.2 gProtein: 19.4 gFiber: 0.3 g

Chicken Nuggets

Servings: 4
Cooking Time: 24 Minutes
Ingredients:

- 1-pound chicken breast, pastured
- 1/4 cup coconut flour
- 6 tablespoons toasted sesame seeds
- 1/2 teaspoon ginger powder
- 1/8 teaspoon sea salt
- 1 teaspoon sesame oil
- 4 egg whites, pastured

Directions:

1. Switch on the air fryer, insert fryer basket, grease it with olive oil, then shut with its lid, set the fryer at 400 degrees F and preheat for 10 minutes.
2. Meanwhile, cut the chicken breast into 1-inch pieces, pat them dry, place the chicken pieces in a bowl, sprinkle with salt and oil and toss until well coated.
3. Place flour in a large plastic bag, add ginger and chicken, seal the bag and turn it upside down to coat the chicken with flour evenly.
4. Place egg whites in a bowl, whisk well, then add coated chicken and toss until well coated.
5. Place sesame seeds in a large plastic bag, add chicken pieces in it, seal the bag and turn it upside down to coat the chicken with sesame seeds evenly.
6. Open the fryer, add chicken nuggets in it in a single layer, spray with oil, close with its lid and cook for 12 minutes until nicely golden and cooked, turning the chicken nuggets and spraying with oil halfway through.
7. When air fryer beeps, open its lid, transfer chicken nuggets onto a serving plate and fry the remaining chicken nuggets in the same manner.
8. Serve straight away.

Nutrition Info:

- InfoCalories: 312 CalCarbs: 9 gFat: 15 gProtein: 33.6 gFiber: 5 g

Cheesy Pork Chops In Air Fryer

Servings: 2
Cooking Time:8 Minutes
Ingredients:

- 4 lean pork chops
- Salt: half tsp.
- Garlic powder: half tsp.
- Shredded cheese: 4 tbsp.
- Chopped cilantro

Directions:

1. Let the air fryer preheat to 350 degrees.
2. With garlic, cilantro, and salt, rub the pork chops. Put in the air fryer. Let it cook for four minutes. Flip them and cook for two minutes more.
3. Add cheese on top of them and cook for another two minutes or until the cheese is melted.
4. Serve with salad greens.

Nutrition Info:

- Info Calories: 467kcal | Protein: 61g | Fat: 22g | Saturated Fat: 8g |

Tasty Harissa Chicken

Servings: 4

Cooking Time:x

Ingredients:

- 1 lb chicken breasts, skinless and boneless
- 1/2 tsp ground cumin
- 1 cup harissa sauce
- 1/4 tsp garlic powder
- 1/2 tsp kosher salt

Directions:

1. Season chicken with garlic powder, cumin, and salt.
2. Place chicken to the slow cooker.
3. Pour harissa sauce over the chicken.
4. Cover slow cooker with lid and cook on low for 4 hours.
5. Remove chicken from slow cooker and shred using a fork.
6. Return shredded chicken to the slow cooker and stir well.
7. Serve and enjoy.

Nutrition Info:

- InfoCalories: 235 Fat: 13g Carbohydrates: 1g Protein: 2Sugar: 1gCholesterol: 130mg

Pork Tenderloin With Mustard Glazed

Servings: 4

Cooking Time:18 Minutes

Ingredients:

- Yellow mustard: ¼ cup
- One pork tenderloin
- Salt: ¼ tsp
- Honey: 3 Tbsp.
- Freshly ground black pepper: ⅛ tsp
- Minced garlic: 1 Tbsp.
- Dried rosemary: 1 tsp
- Italian seasoning: 1 tsp

Directions:

1. With a knife, cut the top of pork tenderloin. Add garlic (minced) in the cuts. Then sprinkle with kosher salt and pepper.
2. In a bowl, add honey, mustard, rosemary, and Italian seasoning mix until combined. Rub this mustard mix all over pork.
3. Let it marinate in the refrigerator for at least two hours.
4. Put pork tenderloin in the air fryer basket. Cook for 18-20 minutes at 400 F. with an instant-read thermometer internal temperature of pork should be 145 F
5. Take out from the air fryer and serve with a side of salad.

Nutrition Info:

- Info Calories: 390 | Carbohydrates: 11g | Protein: 59g | Fat: 11g |

Air Fryer Hen Wings

Servings: 4

Cooking Time: 15 Minutes

Ingredients:

- 6 Chicken Wings - Flats and Drumettes
- Olive Oil Spray
- Salt
- Pepper
- Barbecue Sauce

Directions:

1. Splash the air fryer basket or foil-lined air fryer basket with non-stick cooking spray.
2. Arrange the wings equally into the basket. In a 4-quart air fryer basket, 6 wings fit well. Readjust this as required for the dimension of your air fryer.
3. Include an even layer of olive oil spray, a dashboard of salt, and pepper to the wings.
4. Prepare at 390° for 10 minutes.
5. Turn and also cook for an extra 10 minutes at 390 levels.
6. Make certain the internal temperature of the wings goes to the very least 165°.
7. Coat with BBQ sauce if you prefer or other dipping sauces.

Nutrition Info:

- Info Calories: 308 kcal; Protein:17 g; Fat:11 g; Carbs: 0g

Air Fryer Bbq Cheddar- Stuffed Hen Breasts

Servings: 2

Cooking Time: 25 Minutes

Ingredients:

- 3 strips separated bacon
- 2 oz. cubed and divided Cheddar cheese
- 1/4 cup separated barbeque sauce
- 4 oz. Skinless, boneless hen breasts.
- Salt and ground black pepper

Directions:

1. Cook 1 strip of bacon in the air fryer for 2 minutes. Line the air fryer basket with parchment paper and increase the temperature to 400F.
2. Combine prepared bacon, Cheddar cheese, and also 1 tbsp. barbeque sauce in a bowl.
3. Cover continuing to be strips of bacon around each chicken bust. Coat the breast with remaining barbeque sauce and set into the ready air fryer basket
4. Cook for 10 mins in the air fryer, turn, and also proceed cooking till chicken is no more pink in the facility as well as the juices run clear, about 10 even more minutes.
5. An instant-read thermostat placed into the facility needs to check out at least 165 F.

Nutrition Info:

- Info Calories: 379 kcal; Carbs:12.3g; Protein:37.7g; Fat: 18.9g

Crispy Chicken Thighs

Servings: 2

Cooking Time: 20 Minutes

Ingredients:

- chicken thighs, skin on, bone removed, pat dry
- salt
- garlic powder
- black pepper

Directions:

1. Preheat the Air Fryer to 4000F. Season the chicken with salt and pepper. Place the chicken in the Air Fryer basket.
2. Cook at 4000F for 18 minutes and top with black pepper.
3. Serve.

Nutrition Info:

- Info Calories: 104 kcal; Protein: 13.5g; Carbs: 0g; Fat: 5.7g

Chicken Wings

Servings: 4

Cooking Time: 1 Hour And 30 Minutes

Ingredients:

- 3 pounds chicken wing parts, pastured
- 1 tablespoon old bay seasoning
- 1 teaspoon lemon zest
- 3/4 cup potato starch
- 1/2 cup butter, unsalted, melted

Directions:

1. Switch on the air fryer, insert fryer basket, grease it with olive oil, then shut with its lid, set the fryer at 360 degrees F and preheat for 5 minutes.
2. Meanwhile, pat dry chicken wings and then place them in a bowl.
3. Stir together seasoning and starch, add to chicken wings and stir well until evenly coated.
4. Open the fryer, add chicken wings in it in a single layer, close with its lid and cook for 35 minutes, shaking every 10 minutes.
5. Then switch the temperature of air fryer to 400 degrees F and continue air frying the chicken wings for 10 minutes or until nicely golden brown and cooked, shaking every 3 minutes.
6. When air fryer beeps, open its lid, transfer chicken wings onto a serving plate and cook the remaining wings in the same manner.
7. Whisk together melted butter and lemon zest until blended and serve it with the chicken wings.

Nutrition Info:

- InfoCalories: 240 CalCarbs: 4 gFat: 16 gProtein: 20 gFiber: 0 g

Lemon Pepper Chicken Breast

Servings: 2

Cooking Time:15 Minutes

Ingredients:

- Two Lemons rind, juice, and zest
- One Chicken Breast
- Minced Garlic: 1 Tsp
- Black Peppercorns: 2 tbsp.
- Chicken Seasoning: 1 Tbsp.
- Salt & pepper, to taste

Directions:

1. Let the air fryer preheat to 180C.
2. In a large aluminum foil, add all the seasonings along with lemon rind.
3. Add salt and pepper to chicken and rub the seasonings all over chicken breast.
4. Put the chicken in aluminum foil. And fold it tightly.
5. Flatten the chicken inside foil with a rolling pin
6. Put it in the air fryer and cook at 180 C for 15 minutes.
7. Serve hot.

Nutrition Info:

- Info Calories: 140 | Carbohydrates: 24g | Protein: 13g | Fat: 2g

Crumbed Poultry Tenderloins

Servings: 1

Cooking Time: 12 Minutes

Ingredients:

- 1 egg
- 1/2 mug dry bread crumbs
- 2 tbsps. vegetable oil
- 8 poultry tenderloins

Directions:

1. Adjust the air fryer temperature to 350°F.

2. Blend egg in a small dish. Mix bread crumbs and also oil in a second bowl until the mixture becomes loosened as well as crumbly.

3. Dip each poultry tenderloin into the dish of an egg; get rid of any type of residual egg. Dip tenderloins right into the crumb mix, making sure it is uniformly as well as totally covered. Lay poultry tenderloins right into the basket of the air fryer. Prepare till no longer pink in the facility, about 12 mins. An instant-read thermometer inserted right into the center needs to review at least 165°F.

Nutrition Info:

- Info Calories: 253 kcal; Carbs:9.8g; Protein: 26.2 g. | Fat:11.4 g

Air Fryer Vegetables & Italian Sausage

Servings: 4
Cooking Time:14 Minutes

Ingredients:

- One bell pepper
- Italian Sausage: 4 pieces spicy or sweet
- One small onion
- 1/4 cup of mushrooms

Directions:

1. Let the air fryer pre-heat to 400 F for three minutes.
2. Put Italian sausage in a single layer in the air fryer basket and let it cook for six minutes.
3. Slice the vegetables while the sausages are cooking.
4. After six minutes, reduce the temperature to 360 F. flip the sausage halfway through. Add the mushrooms, onions, and peppers in the basket around the sausage.
5. Cook at 360 F for 8 minutes. After a 4-minute mix around the sausage and vegetables.
6. With an instant-read thermometer, the sausage temperature should be 160 F.
7. Cook more for few minutes if the temperature is not 160F.
8. Take vegetables and sausage out and serve hot with brown rice.

Nutrition Info:

- Info calories 291| fat: 21g| carbs 10g|Protein: 16g

Fried Chicken Tamari And Mustard

Servings: 4
Cooking Time: 1h 20 Minutes

Ingredients:

- 1kg of very small chopped chicken
- Tamari Sauce
- Original mustard
- Ground pepper
- 1 lemon
- Flour
- Extra virgin olive oil

Directions:

1. Put the chicken in a bowl, you can put the chicken with or without the skin, to everyone's taste.
2. Add a generous stream of tamari, one or two tablespoons of mustard, a little ground pepper and a splash of lemon juice.
3. Link everything very well and let macerate an hour.
4. Pass the chicken pieces for flour and place in the air fryer basket.
5. Put 20 minutes at 200 degrees. At half time, move the chicken from the basket.
6. Do not crush the chicken, it is preferable to make two or three batches of chicken to pile up and do not fry the pieces well.

Nutrition Info:

- InfoCalories: 100Fat: 6g Carbohydrates 0gProtein: 18g Sugar: 0g

Chicken Tears

Servings: 4

Cooking Time: 25 Minutes

Ingredients:

- 2 chicken breasts
- Flour
- Salt
- Ground pepper
- Extra virgin olive oil
- Lemon juice
- Garlic powder

Directions:

1. Cut the chicken breasts into tears. Season and put some lemon juice and garlic powder. Let flirt well.
2. Go through flour and shake.
3. Place the tears in the basket of the air fryer and paint with extra virgin olive oil.
4. Select 180 degrees, 20 minutes.
5. Move from time to time, so that the tears are made on all their faces.

Nutrition Info:

- InfoCalories: 197 Fat: 8g Carbohydrates: 16g Protein: 14g Sugar: 0mg Cholesterol: 0mg

Southwest Chicken In Air Fryer

Servings: 4

Cooking Time:30 Minutes

Ingredients:

- Avocado oil: one tbsp.
- Four cups of boneless, skinless, chicken breast
- Chili powder: half tsp.
- Salt to taste
- Cumin: half tsp.
- Onion powder: 1/4 tsp.
- Lime juice: two tbsp.
- Garlic powder: 1/4 tsp

Directions:

1. In a ziploc bag, add chicken, oil, and lime juice.
2. Add all spices in a bowl and rub all over the chicken in the ziploc bag.
3. Let it marinate in the fridge for ten minutes or more.
4. Take chicken out from the ziploc bag and put it in the air fryer.
5. Cook for 25 minutes at 400 F, flipping chicken halfway through until internal temperature reaches 165 degrees.

Nutrition Info:

- Info Calories: 165kcal|Carbohydrates: 1g|Protein: 24g|Fat: 6g

Air Fryer Breaded Pork Chops

Servings: 4
Cooking Time:12 Minutes
Ingredients:

- Whole-wheat breadcrumbs: 1 cup
- Salt: ¼ teaspoon
- Pork chops: 2-4 pieces (center cut and boneless)
- Chili powder: half teaspoon
- Parmesan cheese: 1 tablespoon
- Paprika: 1½ teaspoons
- One egg beaten
- Onion powder: half teaspoon
- Granulated garlic: half teaspoon
- Pepper, to taste

Directions:

1. Let the air fryer preheat to 400 F
2. Rub kosher salt on each side of pork chops, let it rest
3. Add beaten egg in a big bowl
4. Add Parmesan cheese, breadcrumbs, garlic, pepper, paprika, chili powder, and onion powder in a bowl and mix well
5. Dip pork chop in egg, then in breadcrumb mixture
6. Put it in the air fryer and spray with oil.
7. Let it cook for 12 minutes at 400 F. flip it over halfway through. Cook for another six minutes.
8. Serve with a side of salad.

Nutrition Info:

- Info 425 calories|20 g fat| 5 g fiber|31 g protein| Carbs 19g

Chicken Wings With Garlic Parmesan

Servings: 3
Cooking Time: 25 Minutes
Ingredients:

- 25g cornstarch
- 20g grated Parmesan cheese
- 9g garlic powder
- Salt and pepper to taste
- 680g chicken wings
- Nonstick Spray Oil

Directions:

1. Select Preheat, set the temperature to 200 °C and press Start / Pause.
2. Combine corn starch, Parmesan, garlic powder, salt, and pepper in a bowl.
3. Mix the chicken wings in the seasoning and dip until well coated.
4. Spray the baskets and the air fryer with oil spray and add the wings, sprinkling the tops of the wings as well.
5. Select Chicken and press Start/Pause. Be sure to shake the baskets in the middle of cooking.
6. Sprinkle with what's left of the Parmesan mix and serve.

Nutrition Info:

- InfoCalories: 204 Fat: 15g Carbohydrates: 1g Proteins: 12g Sugar: 0g Cholesterol: 63mg

Garlic-roasted Chicken With Creamer Potatoes

Servings:4

Cooking Time:x

Ingredients:

- 1 (2½-to 3-pound) broiler-fryer whole chicken
- 2 tablespoons olive oil
- ½-teaspoon garlic salt
- 8 cloves garlic, peeled
- 1 slice lemon
- ½ teaspoon dried thyme
- ½ teaspoon dried marjoram
- 12 to 16 creamer potatoes, scrubbed

Directions:

1. Do not wash the chicken before cooking. Remove it from its packaging and pat the chicken dry.

2. Combine the olive oil and salt in a small bowl. Rub half of this mixture on the inside of the chicken, under the skin, and on the chicken skin. Place the garlic cloves and lemon slice inside the chicken. Sprinkle the chicken with the thyme and marjoram

3. Put the chicken in the air fryer basket. Surround with the potatoes and drizzle the potatoes with the remaining olive oil mixture.

4. Roast for 25 minutes, and then test the temperature of the chicken. It should be 160°F. Test at the thickest part of the breast, making sure the probe does not touch bone. If the chicken is not done yet, return it to the air fryer and roast it for 4 to 5 minutes, or until the temperature is 160°F.

5. When the chicken is done, transfer it and the potatoes to a serving platter and cover with foil. Let the chicken rest for 5 minutes before serving.

Nutrition Info:

- Info Calories: 491 Fat: 13g Carbohydrates: 1g Protein: 2Sugar: 1gCholesterol: 170mg

Crispy Ranch Air Fryer Nuggets

Servings: 2

Cooking Time: 25 Minutes

Ingredients:

- 1 lb. poultry tenders, sliced into 2-inch pieces
- 1 oz. bundle completely dry cattle ranch salad dressing mix.
- 2 tbsps. flour
- 1 gently beaten egg
- 1 cup panko bread crumbs

Directions:

1. Arrange poultry in a dish, spray with ranch seasoning, as well as toss to integrate. Allow to sit for 10 minutes.

2. Place flour in a resealable bag. Place egg in a little bowl as well as panko bread crumbs on a plate. Adjust the temperature of the air fryer to 391°F.

3. Set poultry into the bag and also toss to layer. Gently dip chicken into egg combination, letting excess drip off. Roll poultry items in panko, pressing crumbs right into the poultry.

4. Spray basket of the air fryer with oil and place chicken items within, making sure not to overlap. You might have to do three batches, depending on the dimension of your air fryer. Gently haze chicken with cooking spray.

5. Cook for 4 minutes. Transform chicken items and also cook until the chicken is not pinker on the inside. Serve.

Nutrition Info:

- Info Calories:244 kcal; Carbs: 25.3g; Protein: 31g; Fat:3.6 g

No-breading Chicken Breast In Air Fryer

Servings: 2
Cooking Time:20 Minutes
Ingredients:

- Olive oil spray
- Chicken breasts: 4 (boneless)
- Onion powder: 3/4 teaspoon
- Salt: ¼ cup
- Smoked paprika: half tsp.
- 1/8 tsp. of cayenne pepper
- Garlic powder: 3/4 teaspoon
- Dried parsley: half tsp.

Directions:

1. In a large bowl, add six cups of warm water, add salt (1/4 cup) and mix to dissolve.
2. Put chicken breasts in the warm salted water and let it refrigerate for almost 2 hours.
3. Remove from water and pat dry.
4. In a bowl, add all the spices with ¾ tsp. of salt. Spray the oil all over the chicken and rub the spice mix all over the chicken.
5. Let the air fryer heat at 380F.
6. Put the chicken in the air fryer and cook for ten minutes. Flip halfway through and serve with salad green.

Nutrition Info:

- Info Calories: 208kcal|Carbohydrates: 1g| Protein: 39g| Fat: 4.5g

Breaded Chicken Tenderloins

Servings: 4
Cooking Time:12 Minutes
Ingredients:

- Eight chicken tenderloins
- Olive oil: 2 tablespoons
- One egg whisked
- 1/4 cup breadcrumbs

Directions.

1. Let the air fryer heat to 180 C.
2. In a big bowl, add breadcrumbs and oil, mix well until forms a crumbly mixture
3. Dip chicken tenderloin in whisked egg and coat in breadcrumbs mixture.
4. Place the breaded chicken in the air fryer and cook at 180C for 12 minutes or more.
5. Take out from the air fryer and serve with your favorite green salad.

Nutrition Info:

- Info Calories 206|Proteins 20g |Carbs 17g |Fat 10g |

Chicken Thighs

Servings: 2

Cooking Time: 20 Minutes

Ingredients:

- 4 chicken thighs
- Salt
- Pepper
- Mustard
- Paprika

Directions:

1. Before using the pot, it is convenient to turn on for 5 minutes to heat it. Marinate the thighs with salt, pepper, mustard, and paprika. Put your thighs in the air fryer for 10 minutes at 3800F

2. After the time, turn the thighs and fry for 10 more minutes. If necessary, you can use an additional 5 minutes depending on the size of the thighs so that they are well cooked.

Nutrition Info:

- Info Calories: 72 kcal; Fat: 2.36g; Carbs: 0g; Protein: 11.78g

Orange Chicken Wings

Servings: 2

Cooking Time: 14 Minutes

Ingredients:

- Honey: 1 tbsp.
- Chicken Wings, Six pieces
- One orange zest and juice
- Worcestershire Sauce: 1.5 tbsp.
- Black pepper to taste
- Herbs (sage, rosemary, oregano, parsley, basil, thyme, and mint)

Directions:

1. Wash and pat dry the chicken wings
2. In a bowl, add chicken wings, pour zest and orange juice
3. Add the rest of the ingredients and rub on chicken wings. Let it marinate for at least half an hour.
4. Let the Air fryer preheat at 180°C
5. In an aluminum foil, wrap the marinated wings and put them in an air fryer, and cook for 20 minutes at 180 C
6. After 20 minutes, remove aluminum foil and brush the sauce over wings and cook for 15 minutes more. Then again, brush the sauce and cook for another ten minutes.
7. Take out from the air fryer and serve hot.

Nutrition Info:

- Info Calories 271 |Proteins 29g |Carbs 20g |Fat 15g |

Chicken Bites In Air Fryer

Servings: 3

Cooking Time:10 Minutes

Ingredients:

- Chicken breast: 2 cups
- Kosher salt& pepper to taste
- Smashed potatoes: one cup
- Scallions: ¼ cup
- One Egg beat
- Whole wheat breadcrumbs: 1 cup

Directions:

1. Boil the chicken until soft.
2. Shred the chicken with the help of a fork.
3. Add the smashed potatoes, scallions to the shredded chicken. Season with kosher salt and pepper.
4. Coat with egg and then in bread crumbs.
5. Put in the air fryer, and cook for 8 minutes at 380F. Or until golden brown.
6. Serve warm.

Nutrition Info:

- Info Calories: 234|protein 25g| carbs 15g|fat 9 g

Beef, Pork And Lamb

Mini Apple Oat Muffins

Servings: 24
Cooking Time: 25 Minutes
Ingredients:

- 1 ½ cups old-fashioned oats
- 1-teaspoon baking powder
- ½-teaspoon ground cinnamon
- ¼-teaspoon baking soda
- ¼-teaspoon salt
- ½ cup unsweetened applesauce
- ¼-cup light brown sugar
- 3 tablespoons canola oil
- 3 tablespoons water
- 1-teaspoon vanilla extract
- ½ cup slivered almonds

Directions:

1. Preheat the oven to 350°F and grease a mini muffin pan.
2. Place the oats in a food processor and pulse into a fine flour.
3. Add the baking powder, cinnamon, baking soda, and salt.
4. Pulse until well combined then add the applesauce, brown sugar, canola oil, water, and vanilla then blend smooth.
5. Fold in the almonds and spoon the mixture into the muffin pan.
6. Bake for 22 to 25 minutes until a knife inserted in the center comes out clean.
7. Cool the muffins for 5 minutes then turn out onto a wire rack.

Nutrition Info:

- Info Calories 70Total Fat 0.7g, Saturated Fat 0.1g, Total Carbs 14.7g, Net Carbs 12.2g, Protein 2.1g, Sugar 2.2g, Fiber 2.5g, Sodium 1mg

Pork Rind

Servings: 4
Cooking Time: 1h
Ingredients:

- 1kg pork rinds
- Salt
- 1/2 tsp black pepper coffee

Directions:

1. Preheat the air fryer. Set the time of 5 minutes and the temperature to 2000C.
2. Cut the bacon into cubes - 1 finger wide.
3. Season with salt and a pinch of pepper.
4. Place in the basket of the air fryer. Set the time of 45 minutes and press the power button.
5. Shake the basket every 10 minutes so that the pork rinds stay golden brown equally.
6. Once they are ready, drain a little on the paper towel, so they stay dry. Transfer to a plate and serve.

Nutrition Info:

- Info Calories: 172 kcal; Fat: 10.02g; Carbs: 0g; Protein: 19.62g

Short Ribs

Servings: 6

Cooking Time: 6 Hours

Ingredients:

- 4 lbs. lean beef short ribs
- 1 tablespoon canola oil
- ¼ cup onion, chopped
- ½ cup celery, chopped
- 3 garlic cloves, minced
- 8 oz. can tomato sauce
- ¼ teaspoon paprika
- ½ teaspoon black pepper

Directions:

1. Heat oil in a skillet over high heat. Add ribs, cook and brown all sides. Add ribs to a slow cooker.
2. Mix the remaining ingredients in a bowl and add over the ribs. Cover and cook for 6 hours on high heat. Serve

Nutrition Info:

- InfoCalories: 769 Fat: 3.41g Carbohydrates: 0g Protein: 20.99g Sugar: 0g

Diet Boiled Ribs

Servings: 4

Cooking Time: 30 Minutes

Ingredients:

- 400 g pork ribs
- 1 teaspoon black pepper
- 1 g bay leaf
- 1 teaspoon basil
- 1 white onion
- 1 carrot
- 1 teaspoon cumin
- 700 ml water

Directions:

1. Cut the ribs on the portions and sprinkle it with black pepper.
2. Take a big saucepan and pour water in it.
3. Add the ribs and bay leaf.
4. Peel the onion and carrot and add it to the water with meat.
5. Sprinkle it with cumin and basil.
6. Cook it on the medium heat in the air fryer for 30 minutes.

Nutrition Info:

- Info Caloric content – 294 kcal Proteins – 27.1 grams Fats – 17.9 grams Carbohydrates – 4.8 grams

Cranberry And Orange Muffins

Servings: 6-8
Cooking Time: 15 Minutes
Ingredients:

- 120g all-purpose flour
- 66g of sugar
- 4g baking powder
- 2g of baking soda
- A pinch salt
- 100g of blueberries
- 1 egg
- 80 ml of orange juice
- 60 ml of vegetable oil
- 1 orange, zest
- Nonstick Spray Oil

Directions:

1. Mix the flour, baking powder, baking soda, salt, and blueberries in a large bowl.
2. Beat the egg, orange juice, oil, and orange zest in a separate bowl.
3. Mix the wet and dry ingredients until well combined.
4. Grease the muffin pans with oil spray and pour the mixture until they are filled to ¾.
5. Preheat the air fryer for a few minutes and set the temperature to 150°C.
6. Place the muffin molds carefully in the preheated air fryer. You may have to work in parts. Set the time to 15 minutes at 150°C.

Nutrition Info:

- InfoCalories: 215 Fat: 0g Carbohydrates: 0g Protein: 0g Sugar: 0g Cholesterol: 17.1mg

Beef Scallops

Servings: 4
Cooking Time: 20 Minutes
Ingredients:

- 16 veal scallops
- Salt
- Ground pepper
- Garlic powder
- 2 eggs
- Breadcrumbs
- Extra virgin olive oil

Directions:

1. Put the beef scallops well spread, salt, and pepper. Add some garlic powder.
2. In a bowl, beat the eggs.
3. In another bowl put the breadcrumbs.
4. Pass the Beef scallops for beaten egg and then for the breadcrumbs.
5. Spray with extra virgin olive oil on both sides.
6. Put a batch in the basket of the air fryer. Do not pile the scallops too much.
7. Select 1800C, 15 minutes. From time to time, shake the basket so that the scallops move.
8. When finishing that batch, put the next one and so on until you finish with everyone, usually 4 or 5 scallops enter per batch.

Nutrition Info:

- InfoCalories: 330 Fat: 3.41g Carbohydrates: 0g Protein: 20.99g Sugar: 0g Cholesterol:1 65mg

Pork Tenderloin

Servings: 6
Cooking Time: 30 Minutes
Ingredients:

- 1-1/2 lbs. pork tenderloin

Directions:

1. Adjust the temperature of the Air Fryer to 3700F.
2. Lay the pork in the Air Fryer basket.
3. Cook at 4000F for about 30 minutes, turning halfway through cooking time for a proper cook.
4. Serve.

Nutrition Info:

- Info Calories: 419 kcal; Fat: 3.5g; Carbs: 0g; Proteins: 26g

Vietnamese Grilled Pork

Servings: 6
Cooking Time: 15 Minutes
Ingredients:

- 1-pound sliced pork shoulder, pastured, fat trimmed
- 2 tablespoons chopped parsley
- 1/4 cup crushed roasted peanuts
- For the Marinade:
- 1/4 cup minced white onions
- 1 tablespoon minced garlic
- 1 tablespoon lemongrass paste
- 1 tablespoon erythritol sweetener
- 1/2 teaspoon ground black pepper
- 1 tablespoon fish sauce
- 2 teaspoons soy sauce
- 2 tablespoons olive oil

Directions:

1. Place all the ingredients for the marinade in a bowl, stir well until combined and add it into a large plastic bag.
2. Cut the pork into ½-inch slices, cut each slice into 1-inches pieces, then add them into the plastic bag containing marinade, seal the bag, turn it upside down to coat the pork pieces with the marinade and marinate for a minimum of 1 hour.
3. Then switch on the air fryer, insert fryer basket, grease it with olive oil, then shut with its lid, set the fryer at 400 degrees F and preheat for 5 minutes.
4. Open the fryer, add marinated pork in it in a single layer, close with its lid and cook for 10 minutes until nicely golden and cooked, flipping the pork halfway through the frying.
5. When air fryer beeps, open its lid, transfer pork onto a serving plate, and keep warm.
6. Air fryer the remaining pork pieces in the same manner and then serve.

Nutrition Info:

- InfoCalories: 231 CalCarbs: 4 gFat: 16 gProtein: 16 gFiber: 1 g

Roast Pork

Servings: 6

Cooking Time: 50 Minutes

Ingredients:

- 2 lbs. pork loin
- 1 Tbsp. olive oil
- 1 tsp. salt

Directions:

1. Adjust the temperature of the Air Fryer to 3600F.
2. Apply the oil on the pork.
3. Add salt.
4. Cook the pork in the Air Fryer for about 50 minutes. Shake the food halfway through the cooking
5. Remove the meal from Air Fryer and allow it to cool.
6. Serve

Nutrition Info:

- Info Calories: 150 kcal; Fat: 6g; Carbs: 0g; Protein: 23.1g

Air Fryer Hamburgers

Servings: 4

Cooking Time:13 Minutes

Ingredients:

- Buns:4
- Lean ground beef chuck: 4 cups
- Salt to taste
- Slices of any cheese: 4 slices
- Black Pepper, to taste

Directions:

1. Let the air fryer preheat to 350 F.
2. In a bowl, add lean ground beef, pepper, and salt. Mix well and form patties.
3. Put them in the air fryer in one layer only, cook for 6 minutes, flip them halfway through. One minute before you take out the patties, add cheese on top.
4. When cheese is melted, take out from the air fryer.
5. Add ketchup, any dressing to your buns, add tomatoes and lettuce and patties.
6. Serve hot.

Nutrition Info:

- Info Calories: 520kcal | Carbohydrates: 22g | Protein: 31g | Fat: 34g |

Cheesy Beef Paseíllo

Servings: 15
Cooking Time: 20 Minutes
Ingredients:

- 1-2 tbsp. olive oil
- 2 pounds lean ground beef
- ½ chopped onion
- 2 cloves garlic, minced
- ½ tbsp. Adobo seasoning
- 2 tsp. dried oregano
- 1 packet of optional seasoning
- 2 tbsp. chopped cilantro
- ¼ cup grated cheese
- 15 dough disks
- 15 slices of yellow cheese

Directions:

1. In a large skillet over medium-high heat, heat the oil. Once the oil has warmed, add the meat, onions, and Adobo seasoning.
2. Brown veal, about 6-7 minutes. Drain the ground beef. Add the remaining seasonings and cilantro. Cook an additional minute. Add grated cheese, if desired. Melt the cheese.
3. On each dough disk, add a slice of cheese to the center and add 3-4 tablespoons of meat mixture over the slice of cheese. Fold over the dough disk and with a fork, fold the edges and set it aside.
4. Preheat the air fryer to 3700C for 3 minutes.
5. Once three minutes have passed, spray the air fryer pan with cooking spray and add 3-4 cupcakes to the basket. Close the basket, set to 3700C, and cook for 7 minutes. After 7 minutes, verify it. Cook up to 3 additional minutes, or the desired level of sharpness, if desired.
6. Repeat until finished.

Nutrition Info:

- InfoCalories: 225 Fat: 3.41g Carbohydrates: 0g Protein: 20.99g Sugar: 0g Cholesterol: 25mg

Pork Liver

Servings: 4
Cooking Time: 15 Minutes
Ingredients:

- 500g of pork liver cut into steaks
- Breadcrumbs
- Salt
- Ground pepper
- 1 lemon
- Extra virgin olive oil

Directions:

1. Put the steaks on a plate or bowl.
2. Add the lemon juice, salt, and ground pepper.
3. Leave a few minutes to macerate the pork liver fillets.
4. Drain well and go through breadcrumbs, it is not necessary to pass the fillets through beaten egg because the liver is very moist, the breadcrumbs are perfectly glued.
5. Spray with extra virgin olive oil. If you don't have a sprayer, paint with a silicone brush.
6. Put the pork liver fillets in the air fryer basket.
7. Program 1800C, 10 minutes.
8. Take out if you see them golden to your liking and put another batch.
9. You should not pile the pork liver fillets, which are well extended so that the empanada is crispy on all sides.

Nutrition Info:

- InfoCalories: 120 Fat: 3.41g Carbohydrates: 0g Protein: 20.99g Sugar: 0g Cholesterol: 65mg

Tuna Wraps

Servings: 4

Cooking Time: 4 To 7 Minutes

Ingredients:

- 1 pound fresh tuna steak, cut into 1-inch cubes
- 1 tablespoon grated fresh ginger
- 2 garlic cloves, minced
- ½ teaspoon toasted sesame oil
- 4 low-sodium whole-wheat tortillas
- ¼ cup low-fat mayonnaise
- 2 cups shredded romaine lettuce
- 1 red bell pepper, thinly sliced

Directions:

1. In a medium bowl, mix the tuna, ginger, garlic, and sesame oil. Let it stand for 10 minutes.
2. Grill the tuna in the air fryer for 4 to 7 minutes, or until done to your liking and lightly browned
3. Make wraps with the tuna, tortillas, mayonnaise, lettuce, and bell pepper. Serve immediately.

Nutrition Info:

- Info Calories: 288 Fat: 7g (22% of calories from fat) Saturated Fat 2g Protein: 31g Carbohydrates: 26g Sodium: 135mg Fiber: 1g Sugar: 1g 152% DV vitamin A 36% DV vitamin C

Stuffed Chicken

Servings: 4

Cooking Time: 30 Minutes

Ingredients:

- 2 chicken breasts
- 2 tomatoes
- 200 g basil
- 1 teaspoon black pepper
- 1 teaspoon cayenne pepper
- 100 g tomato juice
- 40 g goat cheese

Directions:

1. Make a "pocket" from chicken breasts and rub it with black pepper and cayenne pepper.
2. Slice tomatoes and chop basil.
3. Chop the goat cheese.
4. Combine all the ingredients together – it will be the filling for breasts.
5. Fill the chicken breasts with this mixture.
6. Take a needle and thread and sew "pockets".
7. Preheat the air fryer oven to 200 C. Put the chicken breasts in the tray and pour it with tomato juice.
8. Serve.

Nutrition Info:

- Info Caloric content - 312 kcal Proteins – 41.6 grams Fats – 13.4 grams Carbohydrates – 5.6 grams

Roast Beef

Servings:4
Cooking Time: 45 Minutes
Ingredients:

- 1 kg Beef Joint
- 1 tbsp. Extra Virgin Oliver Oil
- Salt
- Pepper

Directions:

1. Rub the beef with extra virgin olive oil.
2. Season with pepper and salt.
3. Then place the seasoned beef onto the air fryer oven rotisserie and put in place.
4. Adjust the timer to 45 minutes and the temperature to 380ºF. Ensure the beef is rotating.
5. After the 45 minutes, check the readiness then slice the roast beef to pieces.
6. Serve

Nutrition Info:

- Info Calories: 666kcal; Protein:43g; Fat:54g

Sirloin Steak

Servings: 6
Cooking Time: 15 Minutes
Ingredients:

- 2 sirloin steaks, grass-fed
- 1 tablespoon olive oil
- 2 tablespoons steak seasoning

Directions:

1. Switch on the air fryer, insert fryer basket, grease it with olive oil, then shut with its lid, set the fryer at 392 degrees F and preheat for 5 minutes.
2. Meanwhile, pat dries the steaks, then brush with oil and then season well with steak seasoning until coated on both sides.
3. Open the fryer, add steaks in it, close with its lid and cook for 10 minutes until nicely golden and crispy, flipping the steaks halfway through the frying.
4. When air fryer beeps, open its lid, transfer steaks onto a serving plate and serve.

Nutrition Info:

- InfoCalories: 253.6 CalCarbs: 0.2 gFat: 18.1 gProtein: 21.1 gFiber: 0.1 g

Light Cheese Cake With Strawberry Syrup

Servings: 4
Cooking Time: 20 Minutes
Ingredients:

- 500g cottage cheese
- 3 whole eggs
- 2 tbsp. powdered sweetener
- 2 tbsp. oat bran
- ½ tbsp. baking yeast
- 2 tbsp. cinnamon
- 2 tbsp. vanilla aroma
- 1 lemon (the skin

Directions:

1. Mix in a bowl the cottage cheese, the sweetener, the cinnamon, the vanilla aroma, and the lemon zest. Mix very well until you get a homogeneous cream.
2. Incorporate the eggs one by one.
3. Finally, add oats and yeast mixing well.
4. Put the whole mixture in a container to fit in the air fryer.
5. Preheat the air fryer a few minutes at 1800C.
6. Insert the mold into the basket of the air fryer and set the timer for about 20 minutes at 180°C.

Nutrition Info:

- InfoCalories: 191 Fat: 12g Carbohydrates: 29g Protein: 4g Sugar: 100g Cholesterol: 7g

Low-fat Steak

Servings: 3
Cooking Time: 10 Minutes
Ingredients:

- 400 g beef steak
- 1 teaspoon white pepper
- 1 teaspoon turmeric
- 1 teaspoon cilantro
- 1 teaspoon olive oil
- 3 teaspoon lemon juice
- 1 teaspoon oregano
- 1 teaspoon salt
- 100 g water

Directions:

1. Rub the steaks with white pepper and turmeric and put it in the big bowl.
2. Sprinkle the meat with salt, oregano, cilantro and lemon juice.
3. Leave the steaks for 20 minutes.
4. Combine olive oil and water together and pour it into the bowl with steaks.
5. Grill the steaks in the air fryer for 10 minutes from both sides.
6. Serve it immediately.

Nutrition Info:

- Info Caloric content – 268 kcal Proteins – 40.7 grams Fats – 10.1 grams Carbohydrates – 1.4 grams

Mediterranean Lamb Meatballs

Servings: 4
Cooking Time: 40 Minutes
Ingredients:

- 454g ground lamb
- 3 cloves garlic, minced
- 5g of salt
- 1g black pepper
- 2g of mint, freshly chopped
- 2g ground cumin
- 3 ml hot sauce
- 1g chili powder
- 1 scallion, chopped
- 8g parsley, finely chopped
- 15 ml of fresh lemon juice
- 2g lemon zest
- 10 ml of olive oil

Directions:

1. Mix the lamb, garlic, salt, pepper, mint, cumin, hot sauce, chili powder, chives, parsley, lemon juice and lemon zest until well combined.
2. Create balls with the lamb mixture and cool for 30 minutes.
3. Select Preheat in the air fryer and press Start/Pause.
4. Cover the meatballs with olive oil and place them in the preheated fryer.
5. Select Steak, set the time to 10 minutes and press Start/Pause.

Nutrition Info:

- InfoCalories: 282 Fat: 23.41 Carbohydrates: 0g Protein: 16.59 Sugar: 0g Cholesterol: 73gm

Russian Steaks With Nuts And Cheese

Servings: 4

Cooking Time: 20 Minutes

Ingredients:

- 800g of minced pork
- 200g of cream cheese
- 50g peeled walnuts
- 1 onion
- Salt
- Ground pepper
- 1 egg
- Breadcrumbs
- Extra virgin olive oil

Directions:

1. Put the onion cut into quarters in the Thermo mix glass and select 5 seconds speed 5.
2. Add the minced meat, cheese, egg, salt, and pepper.
3. Select 10 seconds, speed 5, turn left.
4. Add the chopped and peeled walnuts and select 4 seconds, turn left, speed 5.
5. Pass the dough to a bowl.
6. Make Russian steaks and go through breadcrumbs.
7. Paint the Russian fillets with extra virgin olive oil on both sides with a brush.
8. Put in the basket of the air fryer, without stacking the Russian fillets.
9. Select 1800C, 15 minutes.

Nutrition Info:

- InfoCalories: 1232Fat: 3.41g Carbohydrates: 0g Protein: 20.99g Sugar: 0g Cholesterol: 63mg

Delicious Meatballs

Servings: 6

Cooking Time: 25 Minutes

Ingredients:

- 200 g ground beef
- 200 g ground chicken
- 100 g ground pork
- 30 g minced garlic
- 1 potato
- 1 egg
- 1 teaspoon basil
- 1 teaspoon cayenne pepper
- 1 teaspoon white pepper
- 2 teaspoon olive oil

Directions:

1. Combine ground beef, chicken meat, and pork together in the mixing bowl and stir it gently.
2. Sprinkle it with basil, cayenne pepper, and white pepper.
3. Add minced garlic and egg.
4. Stir the mixture very gently. You should get fluffy mass.
5. Peel the potato and grate it.
6. Add grated potato to the mixture and stir it again.
7. Preheat the air fryer oven to 180 C.
8. Take a tray and spray it with olive oil.
9. Make the balls from the meat mass and put them to the tray.
10. Put the tray in the oven and cook it for 25 minutes.

Nutrition Info:

- Info Caloric content - 204 kcal Proteins – 26.0 grams Fats – 7.6 grams Carbohydrates – 7.1 grams

Air Fried Empanadas

Servings: 2
Cooking Time:20 Minutes
Ingredients:

- Square gyoza wrappers: eight pieces
- Olive oil: 1 tablespoon
- White onion: 1/4 cup, finely diced
- Mushrooms: 1/4 cup, finely diced
- Half cup lean ground beef
- Chopped garlic: 2 teaspoons
- Paprika: 1/4 teaspoon
- Ground cumin: 1/4 teaspoon
- Six green olives, diced
- Ground cinnamon: 1/8 teaspoon
- Diced tomatoes: half cup
- One egg, lightly beaten

Directions:

1. In a skillet, over a medium flame, add oil, onions, and beef and cook for 3 minutes, until beef turns brown.
2. Add mushrooms and cook for six minutes until it starts to brown. Then add paprika, cinnamon, olives, cumin, and garlic and cook for 3 minutes or more.
3. Add in the chopped tomatoes, and cook for a minute. Turn off the heat; let it cool for five minutes.
4. Lay gyoza wrappers on a flat surface add one and a half tbsp. of beef filling in each wrapper. Brush edges with water or egg, fold wrappers, pinch edges.
5. Put four empanadas in an even layer in an air fryer basket, and cook for 7 minutes at 400°F until nicely browned.
6. Serve with sauce and salad greens.

Nutrition Info:

- Info per serving Calories 343 |Fat 19g |Protein 18g |Carbohydrate 12.9g

Salmon Spring Rolls

Servings: 4
Cooking Time: 8 To 10 Minutes
Ingredients:

- ½ pound salmon fillet
- 1 teaspoon toasted sesame oil
- 1 onion, sliced
- 8 rice paper wrappers
- 1 yellow bell pepper, thinly sliced
- 1 carrot, shredded
- ⅓ cup chopped fresh flat-leaf parsley
- ¼ cup chopped fresh basil

Directions:

1. Put the salmon in the air fryer basket and drizzle with the sesame oil. Add the onion. Air-fry for 8 to 10 minutes, or until the salmon just flakes when tested with a fork and the onion is tender.
2. Meanwhile, fill a small shallow bowl with warm water. One at a time, dip the rice paper wrappers into the water and place on a work surface.
3. Top each wrapper with one-eighth each of the salmon and onion mixture, yellow bell pepper, carrot, parsley, and basil. Roll up the wrapper, folding in the sides, to enclose the ingredients.
4. If you like, bake in the air fryer at 380°F for 7 to 9 -minutes, until the rolls are crunchy. Cut the rolls in half to serve.

Nutrition Info:

- Info Calories: 95 Fat: 2g (19% of calories from fat) Saturated Fat: 0g Protein: 13g Carbohydrates: 8g Sodium: 98mg Fiber: 2g Sugar: 2g 73% DV vitamin A 158% DV vitamin C

Potatoes With Loin And Cheese

Servings: 4

Cooking Time: 30 Minutes

Ingredients:

- 1kg of potatoes
- 1 large onion
- 1 piece of roasted loin
- Extra virgin olive oil
- Salt
- Ground pepper
- Grated cheese

Directions:

1. Peel the potatoes, cut the cane, wash, and dry.
2. Put salt and add some threads of oil, we bind well.
3. Pass the potatoes to the basket of the air fryer and select 1800C, 20 minutes.
4. Meanwhile, in a pan, put some extra virgin olive oil, add the peeled onion, and cut into julienne.
5. When the onion is transparent, add the chopped loin.
6. Sauté well and pepper.
7. Put the potatoes on a baking sheet.
8. Add the onion with the loin.
9. Cover with a layer of grated cheese.
10. Bake a little until the cheese takes heat and melts.

Nutrition Info:

- InfoCalories: 332 Fat: 3.41g Carbohydrates: 0g Protein: 20.99g Sugar: 0g Cholesterol: 0mg

Beef With Mushrooms

Servings: 4

Cooking Time: 40 Minutes

Ingredients:

- 300 g beef
- 150 g mushrooms
- 1 onion
- 1 teaspoon olive oil
- 100 g vegetable broth
- 1 teaspoon basil
- 1 teaspoon chili
- 30 g tomato juice

Directions:

1. For this recipe, you should take a solid piece of beef. Take the beef and pierce the meat with a knife.
2. Rub it with olive oil, basil, and chili and lemon juice.
3. Chop the onion and mushrooms and pour it with vegetable broth.
4. Cook the vegetables for 5 minutes.
5. Take a big tray and put the meat in it. Add vegetable broth to the tray too. It will make the meat juicy.
6. Preheat the air fryer oven to 180 C and cook it for 35 minutes.

Nutrition Info:

- Info Caloric content – 175 kcal Proteins – 24.9 grams Fats – 6.2 grams Carbohydrates – 4.4 grams

Fish And Seafood

Sesame Seeds Coated Tuna

Servings: 2

Cooking Time: 6 Minutes

Ingredients:

- 1 egg white
- 1/4 cup white sesame seeds
- 1 tbsp. black sesame seeds
- Salt and ground black pepper
- 6-oz. tuna steaks

Directions:

1. In a shallow bowl, beat the egg white.
2. In another bowl, mix the sesame seeds, salt, and black pepper.
3. Dip the tuna steaks into the egg white and then coat with the sesame seeds mixture.
4. Press the "power button" of air fry oven and turn the dial to select the "air fry" mode.
5. Press the time button and again turn the dial to set the cooking time to 6 minutes.
6. Now push the temp button and rotate the dial to set the temperature at 400ºF.
7. Press the "start/pause" button to start.
8. When the unit beeps to show that it is preheated, open the lid.
9. Arrange the tuna steaks in greased "air fry basket" and insert in the oven.
10. Flip the tuna steaks once halfway through.
11. Serve hot.

Nutrition Info:

- Info Calories: 450 kcal; Fat: 21.9g; Carbs: 5.4g; Protein: 56.7g

Scallops With Creamy Tomato Sauce

Servings: 2

Cooking Time:10 Minutes

Ingredients:

- Sea scallops eight jumbo
- Tomato Paste: 1 tbsp.
- Chopped fresh basil one tablespoon
- 3/4 cup of low-fat Whipping Cream
- Kosher salt half teaspoon
- Ground Freshly black pepper half teaspoon
- Minced garlic 1 teaspoon
- Frozen Spinach, thawed half cup
- Oil Spray

Directions:

1. Take a seven-inch pan (heatproof) and add spinach in a single layer at the bottom
2. Rub olive oil on both sides of scallops, season with kosher salt and pepper.
3. on top of the spinach, place the seasoned scallops
4. Put the pan in the air fryer and cook for ten minutes at 350F, until scallops are cooked completely, and internal temperature reaches 135F.
5. Serve immediately.

Nutrition Info:

- Info Calories: 259kcal | Carbohydrates: 6g | Protein: 19g | Fat: 13g |

Lime-garlic Shrimp Kebabs

Servings: 2

Cooking Time:18 Minutes

Ingredients:

- One lime
- Raw shrimp: 1 cup
- Salt: 1/8 teaspoon
- 1 clove of garlic
- Freshly ground black pepper

Directions:

1. In water, let wooden skewers soak for 20 minutes.
2. Let the Air fryer preheat to 350F.
3. In a bowl, mix shrimp, minced garlic, lime juice, kosher salt, and pepper
4. Add shrimp on skewers.
5. Place skewers in the air fryer, and cook for 8 minutes. Turn halfway over.
6. Top with cilantro and serve with your favorite dip.

Nutrition Info:

- Info Calories: 76kcal | Carbohydrates: 4g | Protein: 13g |fat 9 g

Air-fried Fish Nuggets

Servings: 4

Cooking Time:10 Minutes

Ingredients:

- Fish fillets in cubes: 2 cups(skinless)
- 1 egg, beaten
- Flour: 5 tablespoons
- Water: 5 tablespoons
- Kosher salt and pepper to taste
- Breadcrumbs mix
- Smoked paprika: 1 tablespoon
- Whole wheat breadcrumbs: ¼ cup
- Garlic powder: 1 tablespoon

Directions:

1. Season the fish cubes with kosher salt and pepper.
2. In a bowl, add flour and gradually add water, mixing as you add.
3. Then mix in the egg. And keep mixing but do not over mix.
4. Coat the cubes in batter, then in the breadcrumb mix. Coat well
5. Place the cubes in a baking tray and spray with oil.
6. Let the air fryer preheat to 200 C.
7. Place cubes in the air fryer and cook for 12 minutes or until well cooked and golden brown.
8. Serve with salad greens.

Nutrition Info:

- Info Cal 184.2|Protein: 19g| Total Fat: 3.3 g| Net Carb: 10g

Honey-glazed Salmon

Servings: 2
Cooking Time:15 Minutes
Ingredients:

- Gluten-free Soy Sauce: 6 tsp
- Salmon Fillets: 2 pcs
- Sweet rice wine: 3 tsp
- Water: 1 tsp
- Honey: 6 tbsp.

Directions:

1. In a bowl, mix sweet rice wine, soy sauce, honey, and water.
2. Set half of it aside.
3. In the half of it, marinate the fish and let it rest for two hours.
4. Let the air fryer preheat to 180 C
5. Cook the fish for 8 minutes, flip halfway through and cook for another five minutes.
6. Baste the salmon with marinade mixture after 3 or 4 minutes.
7. The half of marinade, pour in a saucepan reduce to half, serve with a sauce.

Nutrition Info:

- Info calories 254| carbs 9.9 g| fat 12 g| protein 20 g|

Air Fried Cajun Salmon

Servings: 1
Cooking Time:20 Minutes
Ingredients:

- Fresh salmon: 1 piece
- Cajun seasoning: 2 tbsp.
- Lemon juice.

Directions:

1. Let the air fryer preheat to 180 C.
2. Pat dry the salmon fillet. Rub lemon juice and Cajun seasoning over the fish fillet.
3. Place in the air fryer, cook for 7 minutes. Serve with salad greens and lime wedges.

Nutrition Info:

- Info 216 Cal| total fat 19g |carbohydrates 5.6g |protein 19.2g

Fish Finger Sandwich

Servings: 3
Cooking Time:20 Minutes
Ingredients:

- Greek yogurt: 1 tbsp.
- Cod fillets: 4, without skin
- Flour: 2 tbsp.
- Whole-wheat breadcrumbs: 5 tbsp.
- Kosher salt and pepper to taste
- Capers: 10–12
- Frozen peas: 3/4 cup
- Lemon juice

Directions:

1. Let the air fryer preheat.
2. Sprinkle kosher salt and pepper on the cod fillets, and coat in flour, then in breadcrumbs
3. Spray the fryer basket with oil. Put the cod fillets in the basket.
4. Cook for 15 minutes at 200 C.
5. In the meantime, cook the peas in boiling water for a few minutes. Take out from the water and blend with Greek yogurt, lemon juice, and capers until well combined.
6. On a bun, add cooked fish with pea puree. Add lettuce and tomato.

Nutrition Info:

- Info Cal 240| Fat: 12g| Net Carbs: 7g| Protein: 20g

Grilled Salmon With Lemon

Servings: 4

Cooking Time:20 Minutes

Ingredients:

- Olive oil: 2 tablespoons
- Two Salmon fillets
- Lemon juice
- Water: 1/3 cup
- Gluten-free light soy sauce: 1/3 cup
- Honey: 1/3 cup
- Scallion slices
- Cherry tomato
- Freshly ground black pepper, garlic powder, kosher salt to taste

Directions:

1. Season salmon with pepper and salt
2. In a bowl, mix honey, soy sauce, lemon juice, water, oil. Add salmon in this marinade and let it rest for least two hours.
3. Let the air fryer preheat at 180°C
4. Place fish in the air fryer and cook for 8 minutes.
5. Move to a dish and top with scallion slices.

Nutrition Info:

- Info Cal 211| fat 9g |protein 15g| carbs 4.9g

Salmon Cakes In Air Fryer

Servings:2

Cooking Time:10 Minutes

Ingredients:

- Fresh salmon fillet 8 oz.
- Egg 1
- Salt 1/8 tsp
- Garlic powder ¼ tsp
- Sliced lemon 1

Directions:

1. In the bowl, chop the salmon, add the egg & spices.
2. Form tiny cakes.
3. Let the Air fryer preheat to 390. On the bottom of the air fryer bowl lay sliced lemons—place cakes on top.
4. Cook them for seven minutes. Based on your diet preferences, eat with your chosen dip.

Nutrition Info:

- Info Kcal: 194, Fat: 9g, Carbs: 1g, Protein: 25g

Salmon Patties

Servings: 1

Cooking Time: 5 Minutes

Ingredients:

- 14.75 oz. salmon.
- 1 egg.
- 1/4 mug diced onion.
- 1/2 mug bread crumbs.
- 1 tsp. dill weed.

Directions:

1. Start by cleaning the fish, eliminate the bones and also skin. Drain it.
2. Blend the egg, onion, dill weed, as well as breadcrumbs into the salmon. Mix well.
3. Shape into patties. Position them in the air fryer. Set the temperature level at 370F. For 5 minutes, after that turn them and also air fry for 5 more minutes.
4. Serve.

Nutrition Info:

- Info Calories: 290 kcal; Carbs: 1.2g; Protein: 27.g; Fat:18.9g

Coconut Shrimp

Servings:4
Cooking Time:30 Minutes
Ingredients:

- Pork Rinds: ½ cup (Crushed)
- Jumbo Shrimp:4 cups. (deveined)
- Coconut Flakes preferably: ½ cup
- Eggs: two
- Flour of coconut: ½ cup
- Any oil of your choice for frying at least half-inch in pan
- Freshly ground black pepper & kosher salt to taste
- Dipping sauce (Pina colada flavor)
- Powdered Sugar as Substitute: 2-3 tablespoon
- Mayonnaise: 3 tablespoons
- Sour Cream: ½ cup
- Coconut Extract or to taste: ¼ tsp
- Coconut Cream: 3 tablespoons
- Pineapple Flavoring as much to taste: ¼ tsp
- Coconut Flakes preferably unsweetened this is optional: 3 tablespoons

Directions:
1. Pina Colada (Sauce)
2. Mix all the ingredients into a tiny bowl for the Dipping sauce (Pina colada flavor). Combine well and put in the fridge until ready to serve.
3. Shrimps
4. Whip all eggs in a deep bowl, and a small, shallow bowl, add the crushed pork rinds, coconut flour, sea salt, coconut flakes, and freshly ground black pepper.
5. Put the shrimp one by one in the mixed eggs for dipping, then in the coconut flour blend. Put them on a clean plate or put them on your air fryer's basket.
6. Place the shrimp battered in a single layer on your air fryer basket. Spritz the shrimp with oil and cook for 8-10 minutes at 360 ° F, flipping them through halfway.
7. Enjoy hot with dipping sauce.

Nutrition Info:
- Info Calories 340 |Proteins 25g |Carbs 9g |Fat 16g |Fiber 7g

Fish Sticks

Servings: 4
Cooking Time: 15 Minutes
Ingredients:

- 1-pound cod, wild-caught
- ½ teaspoon ground black pepper
- 3/4 teaspoon Cajun seasoning
- 1 teaspoon salt
- 1 1/2 cups pork rind
- 1/4 cup mayonnaise, reduced-fat
- 2 tablespoons water
- 2 tablespoons Dijon mustard

Directions:
1. Switch on the air fryer, insert fryer basket, grease it with olive oil, then shut with its lid, set the fryer at 400 degrees F and preheat for 5 minutes.
2. Meanwhile, place mayonnaise in a bowl and then whisk in water and mustard until blended.
3. Place pork rinds in a shallow dish, add Cajun seasoning, black pepper and salt and stir until mixed.
4. Cut the cod into 1 by 2 inches pieces, then dip into mayonnaise mixture and then coat with pork rind mixture.
5. Open the fryer, add fish sticks in it, spray with oil, close with its lid and cook for 10 minutes until nicely golden and crispy, flipping the sticks halfway through the frying.
6. When air fryer beeps, open its lid, transfer fish sticks onto a serving plate and serve.

Nutrition Info:
- InfoCalories: 263 CalCarbs: 1 gFat: 16 gProtein: 26.4 gFiber: 0.5 g

Fish With Maille Dijon Originale Mustard

Servings: 1

Cooking Time: 5 Minutes

Ingredients:

- 4 tsps. Maille Dijon Originale mustard
- 4 thick trimmed cod steaks
- 2 tbsps. Oil
- 1 tbsp. flat parsley

Directions:

1. Adjust the temperature of the Air Fryer to 3500F.
2. Season the trimmed fish.
3. Spray Maille Dijon Originale mustard on the top side of the cod using a pastry brush.
4. Place the fish in the Air Fryer basket.
5. Cook the meal at 4000F for 5 minutes.
6. Once cooked, you can top it with parsley.
7. Serve

Nutrition Info:

- Info Calories: 383 kcal; Fat: 1.8g; Carbs: 3.6g; Protein: 40.9g

Basil-parmesan Crusted Salmon

Servings: 4

Cooking Time:15 Minutes

Ingredients:

- Grated Parmesan: 3 tablespoons
- Skinless four salmon fillets
- Salt: 1/4 teaspoon
- Freshly ground black pepper
- Low-fat mayonnaise: 3 tablespoons
- Basil leaves, chopped
- Half lemon

Directions:

1. Let the air fryer preheat to 400F. Spray the basket with olive oil.
2. With salt, pepper, and lemon juice, season the salmon.
3. In a bowl, mix two tablespoons of Parmesan cheese with mayonnaise and basil leaves.
4. Add this mix and more parmesan on top of salmon and cook for seven minutes or until fully cooked.
5. Serve hot.

Nutrition Info:

- Info Calories: 289kcal|Carbohydrates: 1.5g|Protein: 30g|Fat: 18.5g

Salmon With Brown Sugar Glaze

Servings: 1
Cooking Time: 15 Minutes
Ingredients:

- 2 tbsps. Dijon mustard
- 4 (6 oz.) Boneless salmon fillets
- 1/4 Cup of packed light brown sugar
- Salt
- Ground black pepper

Directions:

1. Adjust the temperature of the Air Fryer to 3750F.
2. Sprinkle the Fryer basket with cooking spray.
3. Apply pepper and salt on the fish then place it in the Air Fryer basket.
4. In a separate small bowl, whisk together brown sugar and Dijon mustard.
5. Coat the fish properly with the mixture.
6. Cook for about 15 minutes.
7. Serve

Nutrition Info:

- Info Calories: 553 kcal; Fat: 9.2g; Carbs: 18.3g; Protein: 28.9g

Lemon Garlic Shrimp In Air Fryer

Servings: 2
Cooking Time:10 Minutes
Ingredients:

- Olive oil: 1 Tbsp.
- Small shrimp: 4 cups, peeled, tails removed
- One lemon juice and zest
- Parsley: 1/4 cup sliced
- Red pepper flakes (crushed): 1 pinch
- Four cloves of grated garlic
- Sea salt: 1/4 teaspoon

Directions:

1. Let air fryer heat to 400F
2. Mix olive oil, lemon zest, red pepper flakes, shrimp, kosher salt, and garlic in a bowl and coat the shrimp well.
3. Place shrimps in the air fryer basket, coat with oil spray.
4. Cook at 400 F for 8 minutes. Toss the shrimp halfway through
5. Serve with lemon slices and parsley.

Nutrition Info:

- Info Cal 140| Fat: 18g |Net Carbs: 8g|Protein: 20g

Mushrooms Stuffed With Tuna

Servings: 4

Cooking Time: 10 Minutes

Ingredients:

- 8 large mushrooms
- 1 can of tuna
- Mayonnaise

Directions:

1. Remove the trunks to the mushrooms and reserve for another recipe.
2. Peel the mushrooms and place in the basket of the air fryer, face down.
3. Cook for 10 minutes at 1600C.
4. Take out and let cool.
5. In a bowl, mix the well-drained tuna with a little mayonnaise, just to make the tuna juicy and compact.
6. Fill the mushrooms with the tuna and mayonnaise mixture.

Nutrition Info:

- Info Calories: 150 kcal; Fat: 6g; Carbs: 1g; Protein: 8g

Breaded Hake

Servings: 4

Cooking Time: 12 Minutes

Ingredients:

- 1 egg
- oz. Breadcrumbs
- 2 tablespoons vegetable oil
- 6-oz. hake fillets
- 1 lemon cut into wedges

Directions:

1. In a shallow bowl, whisk the egg.
2. In another bowl, add the breadcrumbs and oil and mix until a crumbly mixture form.
3. Dip fish fillets into the egg and then coat with the breadcrumb's mixture.
4. Press the "power button" of air fry oven and turn the dial to select the "air fry" mode.
5. Press the time button and again turn the dial to set the cooking time to 12 minutes.
6. Now push the temp button and rotate the dial to set the temperature at 350 degrees f.
7. Press the "start/pause" button to start.
8. When the unit beeps to show that it is preheated, open the lid. Arrange the hake fillets in greased "air fry basket" and insert in the oven.
9. Serve hot.

Nutrition Info:

- Info Calories: 297 kcal; Fat: 10.6g; Carbs: 22g; Protein 29.2g

Crisped Flounder Fillet With Crumb Tops

Servings: 2

Cooking Time: 15 Minutes

Ingredients:

- A cup dry bread crumbs.
- 1 egg defeated.
- 1sliced lemon.
- 4 pieces go to pieces fillets.
- 5 tbsps. grease.

Directions:

1. Brush flounder fillets with vegetable oil prior to digging up in bread crumbs.
2. Preheat the air fryer to 390ºF.
3. Place the fillets on the double layer rack.
4. Cook for 15 minutes.

Nutrition Info:

- Info Calories: 277 kcal; Carbs:22.5g; Protein:26.9g; Fat:17.7g

Salmon

Servings: 2

Cooking Time: 12 Minutes

Ingredients:

- 2 salmon fillets, wild-caught, each about 1 ½ inch thick
- 1 teaspoon ground black pepper
- 2 teaspoons paprika
- 1 teaspoon salt
- 2 teaspoons olive oil

Directions:

1. Switch on the air fryer, insert fryer basket, grease it with olive oil, then shut with its lid, set the fryer at 390 degrees F and preheat for 5 minutes.
2. Meanwhile, rub each salmon fillet with oil and then season with black pepper, paprika, and salt.
3. Open the fryer, add seasoned salmon in it, close with its lid and cook for 7 minutes until nicely golden and cooked, flipping the fillets halfway through the frying.
4. When air fryer beeps, open its lid, transfer salmon onto a serving plate and serve.

Nutrition Info:

- InfoCalories: 288 CalCarbs: 1.4 gFat: 18.9 gProtein: 28.3 gFiber: 0.8 g

Crispy Fish Sandwiches

Servings: 2

Cooking Time:10 Minutes

Ingredients:

- Cod:2 fillets.
- All-purpose flour: 2 tablespoons
- Pepper: 1/4 teaspoon
- Lemon juice: 1 tablespoon
- Salt: 1/4 teaspoon
- Garlic powder: half teaspoon
- One egg
- Mayo: half tablespoon
- Whole wheat bread crumbs: half cup

Directions:

1. In a bowl, add salt, flour, pepper, and garlic powder.
2. In a separate bowl, add lemon juice, mayo, and egg.
3. In another bowl, add the breadcrumbs.
4. Coat the fish in flour, then in egg, then in breadcrumbs.
5. With cooking oil, spray the basket and put the fish in the basket. Also, spray the fish with cooking oil.
6. Cook at 400 F for ten minutes. This fish is soft, be careful if you flip.

Nutrition Info:

- Info Cal 218| Net Carbs:7g| Fat:12g| Protein: 22g

Air Fryer Fish & Chips

Servings: 4
Cooking Time:35 Minutes
Ingredients:

- 4 cups of any fish fillet
- flour: 1/4 cup
- Whole wheat breadcrumbs: one cup
- One egg
- Oil: 2 tbsp.
- Potatoes
- Salt: 1 tsp.

Directions:

1. Cut the potatoes in fries. Then coat with oil and salt.
2. Cook in the air fryer for 20 minutes at 400 F, toss the fries halfway through.
3. In the meantime, coat fish in flour, then in the whisked egg, and finally in breadcrumbs mix.
4. Place the fish in the air fryer and let it cook at 330F for 15 minutes.
5. Flip it halfway through, if needed.
6. Serve with tartar sauce and salad green.

Nutrition Info:

- Info Calories: 409kcal | Carbohydrates: 44g | Protein: 30g | Fat: 11g |

Baked Salmon

Servings: 2
Cooking Time: 10 Minutes
Ingredients:

- 2 (6 oz. each) skinless fillets salmon, boneless
- 1 tsp. olive oil.
- Salt
- Black pepper, ground

Directions:

1. Spray equal amounts of oil to the salmon. Season with pepper and salt.
2. Set the fillets in your air fryer basket. Allow to cook for 10 minutes at 360°F. Enjoy.

Nutrition Info:

- Info Calories: 170g; Fat: 6g; Proteins: 26g; Carbs: 0g

Tilapia

Servings: 2

Cooking Time: 12 Minutes

Ingredients:

- 2 tilapia fillets, wild-caught, 1 ½ inch thick
- 1 teaspoon old bay seasoning
- ¾ teaspoon lemon pepper seasoning
- ½ teaspoon salt

Directions:

1. Switch on the air fryer, insert fryer basket, grease it with olive oil, then shut with its lid, set the fryer at 400 degrees F and preheat for 5 minutes.

2. Meanwhile, spray tilapia fillets with oil and then season with salt, lemon pepper, and old bay seasoning until evenly coated.

3. Open the fryer, add tilapia in it, close with its lid and cook for 7 minutes until nicely golden and cooked, turning the fillets halfway through the frying.

4. When air fryer beeps, open its lid, transfer tilapia fillets onto a serving plate and serve.

Nutrition Info:

- InfoCalories: 36 CalCarbs: 0 gFat: 0.75 gProtein: 7.4 gFiber: 0 g

Air Fryer Shrimp Scampi

Servings: 2

Cooking Time:10 Minutes

Ingredients:

- Raw Shrimp: 4 cups
- Lemon Juice: 1 tablespoon
- Chopped fresh basil
- Red Pepper Flakes: 2 teaspoons
- Butter: 2.5 tablespoons
- Chopped chives
- Chicken Stock: 2 tablespoons
- Minced Garlic: 1 tablespoon

Directions:

1. Let the air fryer preheat with a metal pan to 330F

2. In the hot pan, add garlic, red pepper flakes, and half of the butter. Let it cook for two minutes.

3. Add the butter, shrimp, chicken stock, minced garlic, chives, lemon juice, basil to the pan. Let it cook for five minutes. Bathe the shrimp in melted butter.

4. Take out from the air fryer and let it rest for one minute.

5. Add fresh basil leaves and chives and serve.

Nutrition Info:

- Info 287 Kcal |total fat 5.5g |carbohydrates 7.5g | protein 18g

Other Favorite Recipes

Air-fried Cinnamon Biscuit Bite

Servings:x
Cooking Time:x
Ingredients:

- 2/3 cup of all-purpose flour
- 2/3 cup of whole-wheat flour
- 1/4 teaspoon of ground cinnamon
- 1/4 teaspoon of kosher salt
- 1/3 cup of whole milk
- 1 teaspoon of baking powder
- 4 tablespoons of cold salted butter
- Cooking spray
- 2 cups of powdered sugar
- 3 tablespoons of water

Directions:

1. Cut the cold salted butter into small pieces. Add salt, cinnamon, baking powder, and flour together in a bowl, and whisk them together. Add butter to the mixture and stir it until the mixture is even.

2. Add milk to the mixture, and stir it together until it forms dough balls. Knead the dough on a surface that has some flour. Knead the dough into smooth and cohesive balls. This should take half a minute.

3. Now, you can cut the dough into 16 pieces and gently roll each of them into a smooth ball.

4. Coat air fryer basket with cooking spray. Then, you can cook the dough at 350 degrees F until it puffs up and goes brown. The cooking should be for about 10 to 12 minutes.

5. Now, you can remove the doughnut balls and place them on a wire rack over a foil. Do the same with the other dough balls.

6. To serve people who are not diabetic, you can mix some granulated sugar with water and sprinkle the solution on the doughnut balls.

Nutrition Info:

- Info Unsaturated Fat: 3g Sodium: 67mg Saturated Fat: 4g Protein: 8g Potassium: 4% DV Fiber: 5g Fat: 7g Carbohydrates: 60g Calories: 325 Calcium: 10% DV

Avocado White Bean Sandwich

Servings: 8
Cooking Time: None
Ingredients:

- 2 medium avocado, pitted and chopped
- 1 (15-ounce) can white beans, rinsed and drained
- 2 tablespoons fresh lemon juice
- 1 tablespoon olive oil
- 1 to 2 cloves minced garlic
- Salt and pepper
- 8 slices whole-wheat or whole-grain bread
- 4 slices low-fat cheddar cheese
- 4 leaves romaine lettuce, halved

Directions:

1. Combine the avocado, white beans, lemon juice, olive oil, and garlic in a medium bowl.

2. Mash the ingredients together with a fork then season with salt and pepper to taste.

3. Toast the slices of bread to your liking.

4. Spread the avocado white bean mixture on the slices of toast.

5. Top each with a half slice of cheese and a lettuce leaf to serve.

Nutrition Info:

- Info Calories 125, Total Fat 3.6g, Saturated Fat 0.5g, Total Carbs 17.2g, Net Carbs 13.6g, Protein 6.4g, Sugar 7.8gFiber 3.6g, Sodium 385mg

Air Fryer Chips

Servings: 2
Cooking Time: 29 Minutes
Ingredients:
- 500 g potatoes.
- 1 tbsp. olive oil.
- 1 pinch sea salt and black pepper.
- 1 tbsp garlic granules.

Directions:
1. Chop the potatoes into slim fries.
2. Place them in a big dish with the oil, salt, pepper, and garlic and also blend well.
3. Put them into the air fryer.
4. Press setting number 1 for the chip set as well as cook for 29 minutes.

Nutrition Info:
- Info Calories: 220 kcal; Carbs: 34g; Protein: 7g; Fat: 1g

Turkey Juicy Breast Tenderloin

Servings: 3
Cooking Time:25 Minutes
Ingredients:
- Turkey breast tenderloin: one-piece
- Thyme: half tsp.
- Sage: half tsp.
- Paprika: half tsp.
- Pink salt: half tsp.
- Freshly ground black pepper: half tsp.

Directions:
1. Let the air fryer preheat to 350 F
2. In a bowl, mix all the spices and herbs, rub it all over the turkey.
3. Spray oil on the air fryer basket. Put the turkey in the air fryer and let it cook at 350 F for 25 minutes, flip halfway through.
4. Serve with your favorite salad.

Nutrition Info:
- Info Calories: 162kcal | Carbohydrates: 1g | Protein: 13g | Fat: 1g |

Shrimp Spring Rolls With Sweet Chili Sauce

Servings:x
Cooking Time:x
Ingredients:

- 8 spring roll wrappers
- 4 ounces of peeled, deveined raw shrimp, chopped
- 3/4 cup of julienne-cut snow peas
- 2 teaspoons of fish sauce
- 2 cups of pre-shredded cabbage
- 2 1/2 tablespoons of sesame oil
- 1/4 teaspoon of crushed red pepper
- 1/4 cup of chopped fresh cilantro
- 1/2 cup of sweet chili sauce
- 1 tablespoon of fresh lime juice
- 1 cup of matchstick carrots
- 1 cup of julienne-cut red bell pepper

Directions:

1. Heat 1 ½ teaspoon of oil and add the bell pepper, carrots, and cabbage to the oil and stir the mixture until the cabbage begins to wilt in less than 2 minutes. Spread the mixture on the baking sheet and allow it to cool for 5 minutes.

2. Add the crushed red pepper, fish sauce, lime juice, cilantro, snow peas, and shrimp to the fried cabbage mixture. Toss them together.

3. Spread the spring roll wrappers and fill them with the mixture. Fold the rolls from left to right corners over the filling. Brush the corners with water.

4. Now, brush the rolls with the remaining oil.

5. The next step is to air fry the spring rolls at 390 degrees F for about 5 minutes. Turn them over before cooking them for another 2 minutes. Serve with sweet chili sauce.

Nutrition Info:

- Info Calories: 180 Total Fat: 9g Protein: 7g Carbohydrates: 19g Fiber: 3g Sodium; 318mg Calcium: 7% DV Potassium: 8% DV

Air Fryer Brussels Sprouts

Servings: 1
Cooking Time: 18 Minutes
Ingredients:

- 2 cups halved brussels sprouts
- 1 tbsp. olive oil.
- 1/4 tsp. sea salt.

Directions:

1. Preheat air fryer to 375°F for 5 minutes.
2. Toss the sprouts in bowl with olive oil as well as add to the air fryer.
3. Gently spray the basket with olive oil cooking spray. Add the sprouts and also cook for 9 mins or to your desired level of crunchy.
4. Salt finished sprouts to taste.

Nutrition Info:

- Info Calories: 50 kcal; Carbs: 4g; Protein:1g; Fat:4g

Creamy Halibut

Servings: 6

Cooking Time: 20 Minutes

Ingredients:

- 2 lbs. halibut fillets cut into 6 pieces
- 1 tsp. dried dill weed
- 1/2 cup light sour cream
- 1/2 cup light mayonnaise
- 4 chopped green onions

Directions:

1. Adjust the temperature of the air fryer to 390°F.
2. Season the halibut with salt and pepper.
3. Mix the onions, sour cream, mayonnaise, and dill in a bowl.
4. Spread the onion mixture evenly over the halibut fillets. Cook in the air fryer for 20 minutes. Serve warm.

Nutrition Info:

- Info Calories: 286 kcal; Fat: 11.3g; Carbs: 6.9g; Protein: 29.8g

Mushroom Barley Risotto

Servings: 8

Cooking Time: 25 Minutes

Ingredients:

- 4 cups fat-free beef broth
- 2 tablespoons olive oil
- 1 small onion, diced well
- 2 cloves minced garlic
- 8 ounces thinly sliced mushrooms
- ¼ tsp. dried thyme
- Salt and pepper
- 1 cup pearled barley
- ½ cup dry white wine

Directions:

1. Heat the beef broth in a medium saucepan and keep it warm.
2. Heat the oil in a large, deep skillet over medium heat.
3. Add the onions, garlic, and sauté for 2 minutes then stir in the mushrooms and thyme.
4. Season with salt, pepper, and sauté for 2 minutes more.
5. Add the barley and sauté for 1 minute then pour in the wine.
6. Ladle about ½ cup of beef broth into the skillet and stir well to combine.
7. Cook until most of the broth has been absorbed then add another ladle.
8. Repeat until you have used all of the broth and the barley is cooked to al dente.
9. Adjust seasoning to taste with salt and pepper and serve hot.

Nutrition Info:

- Info Calories 1555Total Fat 4.8gSaturated Fat 0.7gTotal Carbs 8.5gNet Carbs 4.6g Protein 2.1g Sugar 1.7g Fiber 3.9g Sodium 445mg

Air Fried Steak

Servings: 3
Cooking Time: 12 Minutes
Ingredients:
- 12 oz. strip steaks, 1-inch thick
- Salt
- Pepper
- 2 tbsps. butter

Directions:
1. Set your air fryer to 400ºF.
2. Apply pepper and salt to each side of the steak. Rub with butter and set in air fryer basket without overlapping.
3. Cook for approximately 12 minutes. You can flip halfway.
4. Enjoy.

Nutrition Info:
- Info Calories: 250 kcal; Fat: 17g; Carbs: 0g; Proteins: 23g

Sugar-free Air Fried Chocolate Donut Holes

Servings: 32
Cooking Time: 15 Minutes
Ingredients:
- 6 tbsp. Splenda
- 1 Cup any flour
- Baking Soda: half tsp.
- 6 tbsp. Unsweetened Cocoa Powder
- 3 tbsp. of Butter
- 1 Egg
- Baking Powder: half tsp.
- 2 tbsp. of Unsweetened Chocolate chopped
- 1/4 cup Plain Yogurt

Directions:
1. In a big mixing bowl, combine the baking powder, baking soda, and flour.
2. Then add in the cocoa powder and sugar alternative.
3. In a mug or microwave-safe bowl, melt the butter and the unsweetened chocolate.
4. Mix every 15 seconds and make sure they melt together and combine well.
5. Set it aside to cool it down.
6. In that big mixing bowl from before, add in the yogurt and the egg. Add in the melted butter and chocolate mixture. Cover the bowl with plastic wrap and let it chill in the refrigerator for 30 minutes.
7. To make the donut balls, take out the batter from the fridge.
8. With the help of a tablespoon, scoop out sufficient batter so a donut ball will form with your hands.
9. You can use oil on your hands if the dough is too sticky.
10. Spray the oil on the air fryer basket and sprinkle with flour and let it preheat to 350 F.
11. Work in batches and add the balls in one single layer.
12. Let it bake for 10-12 minutes until they are done. To check doneness, try a toothpick if it comes out clean.
13. Take out from air fryer, let it cool and serve hot or cold.

Nutrition Info:
- Info Calories 22kcal | Carbohydrates: 1g | Protein: 1g | Fat: 2g |

Stir-fried Steak And Cabbage

Servings:4

Cooking Time:x

Ingredients:

- ½-pound sirloin steak, cut into strips
- 2 teaspoons cornstarch
- 1-tablespoon peanut oil
- 2 cups chopped red or green cabbage
- 1 yellow bell pepper, chopped
- 2 green onions, chopped
- 2 cloves garlic, sliced
- ½-cup commercial stir-fry sauce

Directions:

1. Toss the steak with the cornstarch and set aside
2. In a 6-inch metal bowl, combine the peanut oil with the cabbage. Place in the basket and cook for 3 to 4 minutes.
3. Remove the bowl from the basket and add the steak, pepper, onions, and garlic. Return to the air fryer and cook for 3 to 5 minutes or until the steak is cooked to desired doneness and vegetables are crisp and tender.
4. Add the stir-fry sauce and cook for 2 to 4 minutes or until hot. Serve over rice.

Nutrition Info:

- InfoCalories: 180; Total Fat: 7g; Saturated Fat: 2g; Cholesterol: 51mg; Sodium: 1,843mg;Carbohydrates: 9g; Fiber: 2g; Protein: 20g

Shredded Turkey

Servings: 24

Cooking Time: 7 Hours 10 Minutes

Ingredients:

- 4 lbs turkey breast, skinless, boneless, and halves
- 1/2 cup butter, cubed
- 12 oz chicken stock
- 1 envelope onion soup mix

Directions:

1. Place turkey breast into the slow cooker.
2. Combine together butter, chicken stock, and onion soup mix and pour over turkey breast.
3. Cover slow cooker with lid and cook on low for 8 hours.
4. Shred turkey breast with a fork and serve.

Nutrition Info:

- Info Calories 113Fat 5.1 g, Carbohydrates 3.2 g, Sugar 2.7 g, Protein 13 g,Cholesterol 43 mg

Recipe For Eight Flourless Brownies

Servings:x

Cooking Time:x

Ingredients:

- 1/8 teaspoon of salt
- 2 teaspoons of vanilla
- 1 cup of extra virgin coconut oil
- 1 cup of coconut palm sugar
- 1 cup of unsweetened cacao powder
- 4 large eggs

Directions:

1. The first thing is to preheat your oven to about 350F.

2. After that, you can mix all the ingredients listed above thoroughly. Pour the mixture into a parchment paper. Then, bake it in your air fryer for about 25 minutes or a little longer. By then, the brownie may still be soft, but it will have a little jiggle in it. Don't worry about that, just leave it for about 5 hours. It will be a little harder. Then, you can cut and eat your delicious brownies.

3. If you can't wait for up to 5 hours, you can put it in the refrigerator for about 15 minutes to an hour to speed up its cooling. It is also important to remind you that the quantities of the ingredient are for 8 brownies. You may reduce the quantities to make fewer brownies or increase them to make more, but you need to get the hang of it first before you can tweak the quantities.

Nutrition Info:

- Info Potassium: Negligible Calcium: Negligible Sodium: 677mg Fiber: 7g Carbohydrate: 31g Protein: 33g Saturated Fat: 3.5g Unsaturated Fat: 12g Calories: 416

Potatoes With Provencal Herbs With Cheese

Servings: 4

Cooking Time: 20 Minutes

Ingredients:

- 1kg of potatoes
- Provencal herbs
- Extra virgin olive oil
- Salt
- Grated cheese

Directions:

1. Peel the potatoes and cut the cane salt and sprinkle with Provencal herbs.
2. Put in the basket and add some strands of extra virgin olive oil.
3. Take the air fryer and select 1800C, 20 minutes.
4. Take out and move on to a large plate.
5. Cover cheese.
6. Gratin in the microwave or in the oven, a few minutes until the cheese is melted.

Nutrition Info:

- InfoCalories: 437 Fat: 0.6g Carbohydrates: 24.19g Protein: 1g Sugar: 5.g Cholesterol: 0mg

Onion Ring Batter Recipe

Servings:x
Cooking Time:x

Ingredients:

- 1 raw egg
- 2 tablespoons of all-purpose flour
- 2 tablespoons of vegetable oil
- 2 large onions
- 1 cup of milk
- 1 teaspoon of salt
- Additional vegetable oil for frying

Directions:

1. Cut the two large onions into rings and soak the rings in a bowl of ice water. Leave it for up to an hour before you drain and pat them dry with paper towels.

2. Add salt, 2 tablespoons of vegetable oil, milk, and all the all-purpose flour in a bowl. Break the egg into the mixture and whisk them all together until it is very smooth. This won't exceed 5 minutes.

3. Heat the additional vegetable oil either in a large saucepan or in a deep-fryer until the temperature gets to 375 degrees F or 190 degrees C.

4. Now, you can dip the onion rings in the batter one after the other and make sure they are all evenly coated. Arrange them in such a way that a layer will be on a plate.

5. Finally, you have to air fry the battered onion rings in batches until their color turns brown. This will not take more than 5 minutes. After that, you can transfer them to a paper towel-lined plate with a slotted spoon.

Nutrition Info:

- Info 12mg of magnesium Little Vitamin B6 1mg of iron 50mg of calcium 3mg of Vitamin C A little bit of Vitamin A 3g of sugar 4g of protein 1.1g if dietary fiber 18.4g of carbohydrate 314mg of potassium 26mg of cholesterol Saturated Fat 231 calories

Air-fried Pork Dumplings With Dipping Sauce

Servings:x
Cooking Time:x

Ingredients:

- 1 teaspoon of canola oil
- 4 cups of chopped bok choy
- 1 tablespoon of chopped fresh ginger
- 1 tablespoon of chopped garlic
- 4 ounces of ground pork
- 1/4 teaspoon of crushed red pepper
- 18 dumpling wrappers or wonton wrappers
- Cooking spray
- 2 tablespoons of rice vinegar
- 2 teaspoons of lower-sodium soy sauce
- 1 teaspoon of toasted sesame oil
- 1/2 teaspoon of packed light brown sugar
- 1 tablespoon of finely chopped scallions

Directions:

1. Heat the canola oil and add bok choy to it. Cook the mixture for about 6 minutes. Now, add garlic and ginger to the heated mixture while you continue to stir it. Cook it for a minute. Leave the bok choy to cool for 5 minutes before you pat it dry with a paper towel.

2. Mix the crushed red pepper together with ground pork and bok choy.

3. Put some fillings in the dumpling wrappers and fold them into the shape of a half-moon. You may also moisten the edges of the wrappers.

4. Coat your air fryer basket with cooking spray before you place the dumplings in it.

5. Cook at 375 degrees F for about 6 minutes before you turn them over. Cook them for another 6 minutes. When they are done, the dumplings will be browned.

6. Mix the brown sugar, scallions, sesame oil, soy sauce, and rice vinegar together.

7. Serve every 3 dumplings with 2 teaspoons of sauce.

Nutrition Info:

- Info Total Fat: 5g Sodium: 244mg Protein: 7g Potassium: 5% DV Fiber: 1g Carbohydrates: 16g Calories: 140 Calcium: 7% DV

Tahini Oatmeal Chocolate Chunk Cookies

Servings: 8
Cooking Time: 5 Minutes
Ingredients:

- 1/3 cup of tahini
- 1/4 cup of walnuts
- 1/4 cup of maple syrup
- 1/4 cup of Chocolate chunks
- 1/4 tsp of sea salt
- Two tablespoons of almond flour
- One teaspoon of vanilla, it is optional
- 1 cup of gluten-free oat flakes
- One teaspoon of cinnamon, it is optional

Directions:

1. Let the air fryer Preheat to 350 F.
2. In a big bowl, add the maple syrup, cinnamon (if used), the tahini, salt, and vanilla (if used). Mix well, then add in the walnuts, oat flakes, and almond meal. Then fold the chocolate chips gently.
3. Now the mix is ready, take a full tablespoon of mixture, separate into eight amounts. Wet clean damp hands, press them on a baking tray or with a spatula.
4. Place four cookies, or more depending on your air fryer size, line the air fryer basket with parchment paper in one single layer.
5. Let them cook for 5-6 minutes at 350 F, air fry for more minutes if you like them crispy.

Nutrition Info:

- Info Per Servings:Size: 1 cookie: Calories: 185.5| Fat: 11.2g| Carbohydrates: 18.5g| protein 12 g

Air-fried Breakfast Bombs

Servings:x
Cooking Time:x
Ingredients:

- Cooking spray
- 4 ounces of fresh prepared whole-wheat pizza dough
- 3 large eggs
- 3 center-cut bacon slices
- 1 tablespoon of chopped fresh chives
- 1 1/3 ounces less-fat cream cheese, softened

Directions:

1. Lightly beat the eggs.
2. Cook the bacon for about 10 minutes. By then, it will be crispy. Crumble the bacon.
3. Add the beaten eggs to the bacon before cooking the combination for a minute.
4. Transfer the eggs to another bowl before bringing in chives, cream cheese, and the crumbled bacon into the same bowl with the eggs.
5. Divide the dough into 4 equal parts before rolling them up on a surface with flour.
6. Add a quarter of the egg mixture into each piece of the 4 rolls. Brush each roll of dough with water before closing them up on the filling in the shape of a purse.
7. Place all the rolls in your air fryer basket and spray them with cooking spray.
8. Air fry them for 4 minutes before you turn them over.
9. Cook them for another 2 minutes. By then, the rolls will be golden brown in color. You can now serve them.

Nutrition Info:

- Info Calories: 305 Total Fat: 15g Protein: 19g Carbohydrates; 26g Fiber ;2g Sodium: 548mg Calcium: 5% DV Potassium: 2% DV

Spicy Potatoes

Servings: 4
Cooking Time: 30 Minutes
Ingredients:
- 400g potatoes
- 2 tbsp. spicy paprika
- 1 tbsp. olive oil
- cottage cheese
- Salt to taste

Directions:
1. Wash the potatoes with a brush. Unpeeled, cut vertically in a crescent shape, about 1 finger thick Place the potatoes in a bowl and cover with water. Let stand for about half an hour.
2. Preheat the air fryer. Set the timer of 5 minutes and the temperature to 2000C.
3. Drain the water from the potatoes and dry with paper towels or a clean cloth. Put them back in the bowl and pour the oil, salt and paprika over them. Mix well with your hands so that all of them are covered evenly with the spice mixture. Pour the spiced potatoes in the basket of the air fryer. Set the timer for 30 minutes and press the power button. Stir the potatoes in half the time.
4. Remove the potatoes from the air fryer, place on a plate.
5. Serve with cheese and sauce.

Nutrition Info:
- Info Calories: 153 Cal Carbs: 2 g Fat: 11 g Protein: 4 g Fiber: 0 g

Vegetables In Air Fryer

Servings: 2
Cooking Time: 30 Minutes
Ingredients:
- 2 potatoes
- 1 zucchini
- 1 onion
- 1 red pepper
- 1 green pepper

Directions:
1. Cut the potatoes into slices.
2. Cut the onion into rings.
3. Cut the zucchini slices
4. Cut the peppers into strips.
5. Put all the ingredients in the bowl and add a little salt, ground pepper and some extra virgin olive oil.
6. Mix well.
7. Pass to the basket of the air fryer.
8. Select 1600C, 30 minutes.
9. Check that the vegetables are to your liking.

Nutrition Info:
- Info Calories: 135Cal Carbs: 2 g Fat: 11 g Protein: 4 g Fiber: 05g

Air-fried Asparagus

Servings: 4

Cooking Time: 10 Minutes

Ingredients:

- 1/2 bunch asparagus, trim off the bottoms
- Olive Oil
- Salt
- Black pepper, ground

Directions:

1. In your air-fryer basket, add in the asparagus spears. Spray with the olive oil. Season with pepper and salt.
2. Set inside air-fryer and allow to bake for about 10 minutes at 400° F.
3. Serve and enjoy.

Nutrition Info:

- Info Calories: 118.2 kcal; Fat: 8.1g; Carbs: 10.3g; Proteins: 5.2g

Eggplant Fries

Servings: 4

Cooking Time: 20 Minutes

Ingredients:

- 1 eggplant, cut into 3-inch pieces
- 1/4 cup water
- 1 tbsp. olive oil
- 4 tbsps. cornstarch
- Sea salt

Directions:

1. Adjust the temperature of the air fryer to 390°Ft.
2. Mix the eggplant, water, oil, and cornstarch in a bowl.
3. Place the eggplant fries in the air fryer basket, and air fry them for 20 minutes. Serve warm.

Nutrition Info:

- Info Calories: 113.2 kcal; Fat: 7.2g; Protein: 1.9g; Carbs: 12.3g

Crispy Pork Belly Crack

Servings:x

Cooking Time:x

Ingredients:

- ½ teaspoon of pepper
- 1 teaspoon of sea salt
- 1 lb of raw pork belly strips

Directions:

1. Start by slicing the pork belly strips. The idea is to cut the pork into sizes that can be chewed easily.
2. Mix the salt and pepper tighter evenly in a small bowl.
3. Put the pieces of pork belly in the mixture and toss them for even coating.
4. Preheat your air fryer for about 3 minutes
5. Now, put the pieces of pork in your air fryer basket.
6. Set the temperature to about 390 degrees F and cook the pork for about 15 minutes, but make sure you turn them over every 5 minutes.
7. After 15 minutes, they should be crispy and done.
8. Sometimes, they may take a little longer, or they could take less than 15 minutes. That's why you need to keep checking them every 5 minutes.
9. Drain them on paper towels. Now, you can serve them either hot or warm. Enjoy your tasty meal. You can add more spices to yours. Cooking requires being creative.

Nutrition Info:

- Info Protein: 26g Fiber: Negligible amount Carbohydrates: Very small Amount Sodium: 635mg Cholesterol: 95mg Unsaturated Fat:15g Saturated Fat: 9g Total Fat: 24g Calories: 332

Breaded Pork Chops In An Air Fryer

Servings: 4

Cooking Time: 10 Minutes

Ingredients:

- 4 Center-cut boneless Pork chops
- 1 tsp. Cajun seasoning
- 1-1/2 cups Garlic and cheese-flavored croutons
- 2 Eggs
- Cooking spray

Directions:

1. Adjust the temperature of the air fryer to 390°F.

2. Take a plate and transfer the Cajun seasoning to it. Take 1 pork chop and coat it with the seasoning. Make sure both sides are evenly coated. Repeat the process with the remaining chops.

3. In a food processor, pulse the flavored croutons until the consistency is fine. Once done, empty them onto a shallow dish.

4. Take another shallow dish and dip each pork chops into the eggs. Then coat them in the crouton crumble evenly on all sides. Set them aside on a plate.

5. Take the air fryer basket and grease it using the cooking spray. Place 2 chops inside the basket and cook them for about 5 minutes. Flip over the chops and lightly mist them using a cooking spray. Cook for another 5 minutes. Repeat the process with the remaining pork chops.

6. Once done, transfer the cooked chops onto a serving platter and serve hot.

Nutrition Info:

- Info Calories: 400 kcal; Proteins: 44.7 g; Carbs: 10 g; Fat: 18.1 g

Honey Roasted Carrots

Servings:2-4

Cooking Time: 12 Minutes

Ingredients:

- 454g of rainbow carrots, peeled and washed
- 15 ml of olive oil
- 30 ml honey
- 2 sprigs of fresh thyme
- Salt and pepper to taste

Directions:

1. Wash the carrots and dry them with a paper towel. Leave aside.

2. Preheat the air fryer for a few minutes an 1800C.

3. Place the carrots in a bowl with olive oil, honey, thyme, salt, and pepper. Place the carrots in the air fryer at 1800C for 12 minutes. Be sure to shake the baskets in the middle of cooking.

4. Serve hot.

Nutrition Info:

- InfoCalories: 123Fat: 42g Carbohydrate: 9g Protein: 1g

Appendix : Recipes Index

Chicken Bites In Air Fryer 39
Chicken Croquette 20
Chicken Nuggets 29
Chicken Tears 35
Chicken Thighs 39
Chicken Wings 32
Chicken Wings With Garlic Parmesan 36
Chicken's Liver 28
Chickpea, Tuna, And Kale Salad 15
Chinese Chili 23
Coconut Shrimp 56
Cocotte Eggs 10
Cranberry And Orange Muffins 42
Cream Buns With Strawberries 5
Creamy Halibut 66
Crisped Flounder Fillet With Crumb Tops 59
Crispy Chicken Thighs 32
Crispy Fat-free Spanish Potatoes 26
Crispy Fish Sandwiches 60
Crispy Pork Belly Crack 73
Crispy Ranch Air Fryer Nuggets 37
Crumbed Poultry Tenderloins 33

D

Delicious Meatballs 49
Diet Boiled Ribs 41

E

Easy Air Fryer Omelet 17
Eggplant Fries 73

F

Fish Finger Sandwich 54
Fish Sticks 56
Fish With Maille Dijon Originale Mustard 57
French Toast In Sticks 11
Fried Chicken Tamari And Mustard 34

G

Garlic Bread 12
Garlic-roasted Chicken With Creamer Potatoes 37
Green Beans 23
Grilled Cheese 7
Grilled Salmon With Lemon 55

H

Herb Chicken Thighs 28
Herb Frittata 14
Honey Roasted Carrots 74

Russian Steaks With Nuts And Cheese 49

Printed in Great Britain
by Amazon

31352398R00051